The Book of Love

SELECTED TITLES

The Boy Detective

Kayak Morning

Unless It Moves the Human Heart

Making Toast

Beet

Lapham Rising

Children of War

Rules for Aging

Anything Can Happen

The Man in the Water

The Book of Love

IMPROVISATIONS
ON
A CRAZY LITTLE THING

Roger Rosenblatt

An Imprint of HarperCollins*Publishers*

Portions of this book have appeared, in different forms, in *Anything Can Happen,* the *Washington Post,* and *Time* magazine.

HarperCollins books may be purchased for educational, business, or sales promotional use. For information please e-mail the Special Markets Department at SPsales@harpercollins.com.

FIRST EDITION

Designed by Suet Yee Chong

Library of Congress Cataloging-in-Publication Data has been applied for.

ISBN 978-0-06-234942-2

15 16 17 18 19 OV/RRD 10 9 8 7 6 5 4 3 2 1

For Ginny—

Dedicated to the One I Love

The Book of Love

The Chinese invented the clock and gave it to the emperor, who stored it away in his palace. Eventually it was lost, and everyone who knew about the clock forgot about it. Four hundred years later, the French sailed into China, bearing a new invention of theirs, the clock. The Chinese, including the current emperor, were filled with amazement. They murmured and gaped, turning the machine this way and that. They said they never had seen anything as wonderful as a clock.

I thought of you tonight, as the moon was turning its knowing face, the way you turn away at one of my contrived displays of wit. Embarrassed for me, who lacks the wit to be embarrassed for myself. Why is that? Why are you prepared to bear my slightest burden? I, the tropical ceiling fan, wheeling in my faux aristocratic self-confidence. You, with the serene sense to look beyond the slats of the casa shutters to the mango trees, the bougainvillea, and beyond those, to the sea. So steady, your eyesight. But tonight was different. The past had changed, as it does sometimes, and instead of the self-regard I have worn like a white linen suit, I saw only you, and the strawberries, and the windfall of light on your hair.

The story I have to tell is of you. It was related to me by a priest who had read it in an Icelandic saga memorized by an Irishman who recited it on a road packed with flutists and soldiers, where he was overheard by a young girl from Florida who transcribed it in a language no one speaks anymore. So I need to tread carefully. Stories like yours tend to slip away, if one is not careful. And I have been known not to be careful. A dead language is like the ruins of a great civilization. It glows as it is excavated. I shall tell your story in that language, whose power derives from not saying everything, like a poem. Or a song. Maybe a song.

The story I have to tell is of you. Of others, too. Other people, other things. But mainly of you. It begins and ends with you. It always comes back to you.

SWONDERFUL, SBLUNDERFUL, SROMANTIC, frantic, logical, biological, whimsical, flimsical, writerly, golighterly, puppy, yuppie, durable, curable, erratic, ecstatic, erotic, robotic, national, passional, powerful, flowerful, ephemeral, dilemmeral, musical, abusical, tragic, magic, mawkish, New Yawkish, ubiquitous, insickuous, loyal, cloyal, fleeting, cheating, parental, demental, beautiful, dutiful, diurnal, eternal, sawfullynice, sparadise.

THE PIANO BAR PLAYER is trying to express his fondness for the brunette standing near his bench. She has requested "Someone to Watch Over Me," and has pointed out the song in the fake book that the piano player keeps propped up on his music stand. But the fake book is itself a prop. He cannot read music. He cannot tell her that. He wants so for her to like him, and she does. But "Just the Way You Are"? He was riffing on that tune when she entered the lounge. She seems above him, superior to him who never learned to do anything the right way. He is just a piano bar player. How he wants to please and impress her. So he fidgets with the page of music, flutters it, and peers in, as if he were actually studying the chord progressions of "Someone to Watch Over Me." She watches over his shoulder, then touches him on the arm. "Love songs are desire," she says. "Why don't you play it the way you feel it?" At once he relaxes and fails to exist, just as one fails to exist in water lights at the harbor, or in that first bite of a plum, in the summer, on a boat. "Why don't we ride the song like a rainy road at night?" he says to her, courage mounting and the fingering flowing ahead of him, clairvoyant. He recalls the ecstasy of his years of failed instruction, and thinks, I never needed lessons, after all.

Some enchanted evening, you will meet a stranger and call it love at first sight, but it won't be. We say that, love at first sight, when in fact we mean the opposite. In order to love someone you've never laid eyes on before, you need to have retained an impression of the person you would fall in love with once that person materialized. An amalgam, perhaps, of the best features of those you nearly loved. A composite image, like a police sketch. Finally, after many years, when that impression becomes a reality, and that person comes into view, across a crowded room or in a piano bar, or whatever, then somehow you know, because you always had known. Your imagination has preserved a picture of the love of your life. And look at *that,* she appears. So, when you think about it, the expression *love at first sight* really means "love at last." Now that you know that, you can run to her side and make her your own. There you go.

Things I can take, things I can't.

I can take a punch. Maybe not two punches or three. But one, to the belly or the face. I can take a punch.

And a snub. I've been snubbed a lot, so I know that I can take a snub. Walk past me here. Don't invite me there. I can take it.

I can take extreme heat and extreme cold. The heat was overwhelming in Lebanon and Israel. I climbed the

Rock of Masada in a hundred degrees, which was no fun. But I could take it. And the cold, too, in Vermont and New Hampshire, those winters when the gas froze in the tank.

And a slur. I can take a slur. Call me kike, Hebe, Jewboy. I can take that, too, though I'd probably want to find out if *you* can take a punch.

Gossips. I can take them, as well. I don't like gossip, but I can live with it. And the company of fakes and tyrants and traitors and amiable accommodators—for brief periods. I can take it.

Disorder. It's difficult for a Virgo. But I can take it. And shocks, I can take shocks. And I can take a joke.

And ingratitude; I kind of expect it. And cheapness and pettiness. Even rejection. I can take that. And an unlucky streak. Treachery, if you must. It gets me down, but I can take it.

Things I can't take: your pain, the children's pain, the verdict of your glance.

FROM TIME TO TIME on the *George Burns and Gracie Allen Show,* a character, perplexed as to how George could be with a scatterbrain like Gracie, would approach George and begin, "I hope you won't mind my asking—" At which point, George would cut him off and say, "I love her."

Jack Benny reported that when Gracie died, hundreds of friends filled George and Gracie's home. George greeted them with a smile, and told jokes to make them laugh. Every twenty minutes or so, Benny said, George would go off to a room by himself and weep. Then he'd return to his company, and make them laugh again.

"I THOUGHT YOU WERE GOING to be there when I died," says the husband in the movie *Take This Waltz*, just as his marriage is about to expire. A morose variant on the cliché "you're the one I wanted to grow old with." The remark is effective, as it comes from this particular husband, who is one of the world's nicest guys. He cooks chicken, and writes cookbooks about cooking chicken. His first published success will be a book called *Tastes Like Chicken*. But that will come after his spritelike wife of five years runs off with another. She has loved her husband in a safe and solid way, because he is safe and solid. He views the future as death. "I thought you were going to be there when I died." But she is neither safe nor solid. She dreams. And when the guy across the street (this is Toronto) catches her eye, she falls in love at first sight, which, as we know, means love at last. She is sort of a writer. He is sort of a painter, who transports citizens of Toronto in a rickshaw to earn a little money. He, too, is a nice guy. There are no villains in this piece.

If the movie is about anything, it is about gaps. Every life has at least one gap. And the choice every husband, wife, and lover makes is to live with one's gap, or try to fill it. When the gap is filled, inevitably a different gap is revealed, just as gaping. "The Folks Who Live on the Hill," that sweet, hopeful song about the safe and solid. How perfect would life be were we to love and wed and have some kids and see our children play and grow till we were old. And we would be called what we have always been called—the folks who live on the hill.

Take this scene in *Take This Waltz*: Before the lovers become lovers, physical lovers, body to body, they take an early morning swim together in a health club pool. They are the only ones in the pool. We watch them move toward and around each other, and away, and close again, but never touching. In an earlier scene he tells her how he would make love to her, up and down, if they were free to do what they wished. They do not touch in that scene, either. After their long aquatic ballet, the guy breaks the spell and grabs her ankle. Her expression changes, hardens. The swim dance is over. And, in fact, when they finally get together after she leaves her husband, they don't last as a couple, because all they really had between them was their swim, a gap of their own, where nothing could go wrong. Only in the pool could their interplay be mistaken for life, the best life available to them, with no marriage vows broken, no taboos violated, and no disappointment. Forever would they be known as the folks who live in the water.

On gaps? First, a coffee cup is between you. Then a swimming pool. Then an ocean. Then everything. Keep your eye on gaps. They tend to grow when you're not looking, like orchids, except they're not as pretty as orchids.

Advice to those about to acquire a Vermeer: Always look at it as it might appear in its average moments—not as it might glow in the light-dance of the fireplace, or burn from within on a fall Sunday morning when the amalgamation of the sun's rays blasts red upon those fat Dutch cheeks, or as you would make it glow when you return home flushed with the one victory or another, or with wine. None of that.

Rather think: What will this masterpiece look like at 2:45 on a February afternoon when you have run out of toilet paper and the roof leaks and a horse has just kicked in your kitchen door for the fun of it. And a dead badger is wedged high in the chimney, stinking up the house. Consider moments such as these, when you are about to acquire your Vermeer. But yes. She *is* as lovely as a Vermeer.

There is something you should know. Uh-oh. I went and said it. There is something you should know. Your face stiffens. Your lips go dry. You seem certain that you are about to learn something painful, a terrible secret. Another woman? Another man? There is something you should know. One might as well say, I am about to ruin your life.

But think on it a moment. Just because the announcement usually is dire does not mean it has to be. Every time, I mean. There is something you should know. Say you are about to journey to an unknown place. And I, who have been to that place, would like to prepare you for certain contingencies and customs. At the dinner table, for instance, these people you are about to meet toss their food in the air and let it fall in their mouths. They all are quite good at this trick, and never spill a drop or a morsel. Do not be put off by this, much less horrified. It's just their way. You might practice the trick yourself before you start out on your journey. Something you should know.

Or, the climate plummets below zero in the summers, and cornfields grow so red hot in the winters the corn rises just like that. Or polar bears run wild in the streets, and are deceptively affectionate, often appearing at your door and posing as houseguests. Or the women who live here insist on fornication as a gesture of welcome. Something you should know.

When it comes down to it, there is a lot that you should know if you do not already know it. Thus the announcement may be proffered at face value. If you are about to take a course in trigonometry, you should know algebra. If you are about to perform a quadruple bypass, it helps to know how to do it. Arcana you should know: You should know that the expression "the devil and the deep blue sea" has nothing to do with Satan, but rather refers to the line where a boat rests on the water, called the devil. You should know that "the lion's share" derives from a fable even earlier than Aesop's, in which the lion goes hunting with a cow, a goat, and a sheep, and claims all the spoils. So the phrase means not the largest portion, but rather the whole thing. You should know that the Chinese invented the clock.

And even this: The announcement may augur a delightful piece of news. People are speaking well of you. You should know that. You are about to inherit a fortune, or be awarded a prize. You should know that. You are beloved more than you ever can realize, in all the ways that someone can be loved, from every angle, from every way of looking at you or into you, for every quality of mind and heart that you possess. And for your frailties, too. And insecurities. And for your failings and stumbles. And your sins, for those as well. You are beloved for being, and you need not lift a finger to earn it. Love is yours. My love is yours. Even this is something you should know.

JACK CALLS PAUL A NIGGER FAG, and Paul says the same thing of Jack. Whenever they fight, which is every fourth or fifth day, they will not speak to each other for one whole day afterward, and will fume and seethe and stomp around their railroad apartment on Bleecker Street, murmuring "nigger fag" as they pass each other in the hall. In bed they will roll to the outskirts, back to back with most of the bed in the gap between them. Yet all their friends know them to be "the happiest couple in New York." And much of the time they are. Theirs was one of the first same-sex marriages in the state, and that makes them proud. And basically they are compatible, peas in a pod. They both like cooking and classical music. They like Vermeer. They like reruns of *Burns and Allen*. They like chess. They like baseball. They like pop, too—Blossom Dearie, Barbara Cooke, and Dean Martin, especially "Ain't That a Kick in the Head." And they both like fighting, which seems to come naturally to each of them, as Jack was reared in the South Central district of Los Angeles, and Paul in Bed-Stuy. You can take the boy out of the hood, says Jack, and Paul completes the axiom.

Which is why it was a near-fatal mistake for the six skinheads on Harrison Street one night, when they surrounded Paul and Jack, and called them nigger and called them fag. Both men were dressed in identical powder blue pullovers, and they were returning home from the ad agency that employs them. They must have looked like easy marks to the skinheads who, after a brawl that lasted no more than two minutes, limped away with fat lips and shiners (one with a crushed nose), while Jack and Paul bore hardly a scratch. On the walk home, they whistled "Ain't That a Kick in the Head." Tonight, they are side by side on the couch, watching *Mad Men* in peace and comfort, and holding hands, until Paul drives Jack up the wall by saying he's got a man crush on Jon Hamm, and Jack calls him a nigger fag. Paul says the same thing of Jack.

Should we mix it up this Valentine's Day? I mean, a knock-down-drag-out, no-holds-barred, mano a mano donnybrook? Tell you what. Let's make love instead. Let's do both, and fight between the sheets. Does that make sense? Does anything about love make sense? Love is irrational, delirium, which is why neither of us would want to be one of those gods graced with eternal life, because if you have eternal life, why panic? Where's the fire? But if you're mortal, and are we ever, carpe diem, carpe whatever frantic impulse comes charging through your heart. So, what is it to be, baby? A shot to the kisser, or embraceable you? (I like a Gershwin tune. How about you?) Plant one on me.

The safest place to be in a tornado is a storm cellar. The safest place to be in a tornado is a railroad apartment on Bleecker Street or a Motel 6 or Williams-Sonoma or a bank vault or a North Korean prison. The safest place to be in a tornado is in your arms, you said, and you thought you meant it but you didn't. Love is no safer than a bread knife. Take the storm cellar. Tea for two and two for tea and me for you in a cottage small by a waterfall? I don't think so. Embrace the peril. If we're going to pick our song, let's make it "That Old Black Magic" and revel in the spin we're in.

How do conservatives fall in love? Conservatively, I suppose, like porcupines. Love may be better suited to liberals, for whom disorder is a work of the imagination. Within the blink of a black eye, you can be enthralled by me, disgusted with me, appalled, enchanted, smitten, bored (*Bored*? With *me*?), forever mine, forever through with me. Analyze that. The trick is not to forget that we love each other, because couples do that. They forget to remember. As if love were keys to misplace or a purse to leave in an airport. What? Did I slip your mind? Did you slip mine? My irreplaceable you. My sweet erasable you, you'd be so nice to come home to. That is, you or Tracey the waitress with the boobs I glimpsed in Applebee's last Tuesday. Unforgettable, that's what you are not, unless I concentrate on you.

Pope Francis wants a church "bruised, hurting and dirty because it has been out on the streets" and not "clinging to its own security." Does that make sense? Is the pope Catholic? Francis embraces life as a holy mess. Love is a holy mess. You were not meant for me. I was not meant for you. Yet there we were in the snow, our first night together, the quiet luster of you, composed like a Gershwin tune, like "Embraceable You," while I, a whooping rhinoceros, stomped about in boots, a rhino in boots, until we stopped, stood thigh to thigh, looked up and caught the moon between the tangles of the clouds. My heart fell open like a knot.

Be my valentine in a blizzard, where the air is so thick, we cannot see two feet ahead of us, and we flail about snow-blind, without a GPS. Be my GPS to the tundra, the Klondike, and I'll be yours. The outer world of fanatics hates at the drop of a hat. Let us love as fanatically, unhinged. O promise me nothing. Is that you standing before me in the whiteout? Come to Papa. Do.

THESE DISTRACTED LOOKS OF MINE drive you up the wall, I know. I wish I could help it. No, I don't. Distracted is where I live. For weeks I have been turning a line over in my head—On first looking into Homer's Chapstick. Nothing good can come of such falderal, yet falderal is how I ral. How I roll. A Tootsie Tells How She Rolls. Did you know that Van Gogh's love song was "Call My Ear Responsible"? See? It is unthinkable that a noblewoman such as yourself should stoop to my level.

I talk to birds. Out loud. I talk to birds. In the early

morning, when I am at the kitchen table writing, and a bird lands on top of the hedge outside the glass door to the deck, I talk to it, greet it, often with the single word "Bird." Stirred by a bird. I talk to squirrels, or to one particular squirrel (is it the same one every morning?), who skitters across the deck, sometimes from left to right, sometimes from right to left. In midskitter he will stop in his tracks, distrackted, rear up, and turn to me, as if to say, annoyed, "What?" On the other side of the kitchen wall, you are watching Charlie Rose on *CBS This Morning* lead a discussion of whether or not we should invade Syria.

What would I do if I invaded Syria? Even if Syria deserves an invasion, I'm not familiar with the terrain. I wouldn't know where to go. Out of things. I'm too out of things. I wish I could be more with it, but then I might be conscripted to invade Syria, and how would that be? Who am I kidding? I don't wish I were more with it, neither does it, whatever it may be. You've known me since I was a fledgling distractee. Now I'm a pro. The distraction game can get out of hand, I hardly need to tell you. But on the whole (who sits on the whole?), it's not a bad way to live. And, distracted as I may be, I always turn up, like the bad penny. The bad penny.

The good penny and the bad penny went for a walk. We may be different from each other, they agreed. But neither of us needs change.

Oh, I wonder, wonder who, mmbadoo-ooh, who
Who wrote the Book of Love.

—THE MONOTONES, "THE BOOK OF LOVE"

Well, as long as you're asking, it was Andreas Capellanus who wrote the book of love, at least the first of the lot, called *The Art of Courtly Love,* around 1184. Curious little treatise, it defines love in terms of the "inborn suffering" someone endures when thinking about one's beloved, which is sensible enough. But then the book goes off the rails in a section that condemns homosexuality, while recommending hitting on nuns. Capellanus was a monk. His main theme, courtly love itself, declares that the most satisfying love affair exists between an unmarried man and a married woman, like Troilus and Cressida, and he advocates stealing another man's wife (felonious monk). Then there's a kinky passage comparing a woman's "upper half" to her "lower half," in a bodily exploration similar to the young man's in *Take This Waltz,* but without the heavy breathing. The passage sails into a lengthy dialogue involving a woman who offers two suitors a choice of the halves of her body, and a debate ensues between the suitors as to who gets what. The woman does not ask, why not take all of me? And by the time you finish with all this anatomical chatter, you want no part of any of them.

Yet *The Art of Courtly Love* does offer two things worth

holding on to. Love, says Capellanus, tracing the Latin, gets its name (*amor*) from the word for hook (*amus*). Someone in love is hooked, poor fish. The more he tries to wriggle off the line, the tighter the line. Finally, our odd little monk comes to something you and I might recognize in his prescription for courting a woman of superior social position. He writes: "Where a man is of lower rank than the woman, he must not ask permission to sit beside her, but he may ask to sit in a lower place." I'm down here, babe.

MY BEAR IS OF THE POLAR VARIETY. He squats at the other end of my kitchen table every morning, and he stares at me with his black, black eyes. He does not move, but I hear his even snorting. *Gnnn, gnnn, gnnn.* Like that, in a low guttural snort that is neither threatening nor amiable. If my kitchen window is open, the breeze will flutter the tips of his white fur. He is seven or eight feet tall (I haven't measured). There is nothing immediately alarming about him, yet once I sit down, I am afraid to move.

He has something to do with embracing my fears. Anyone can see that. And with my mood swings. Once I suggested to him that he might be a bipolar bear, but he showed no amusement. I cannot recall when he first appeared—some years ago, certainly. It was not in the morning that I first saw him but rather one midnight, when, for lack of sleep, I came downstairs for a snack of Jell-O, and there he was, glowing white in the light of a full moon. I sat and stared at him, as he stared at me. I blinked first. He did not blink at all. Eventually, I got sleepy and retired.

Lately, he has stirred from the kitchen, where he spends his days, and has moved up to the bedroom at night, where he sits Indian-style at the foot of my bed. He seems to wish to be with me night and day. I do not know what it is about me that attracts him. If he wanted to kill me, he could have done that long ago. Bears may look cute, but they are ferocious. One swipe of the paw, and I would be scattered around the room like so many pieces of paper.

One night I decided to flatter him, but it made no impression. One night I presented a philosophical monologue to him—something that yoked the fates of bears and men together in harmony. I sang him "Can't We Be Friends?" He demonstrated no interest. One night I read him *The Art of Courtly Love*. Ditto. One night I cursed him out. I don't know where I got the courage, but I even raised my hand to him. I hardly need tell you that there was no reaction.

Here's my problem: If he establishes his influence in my household, as he has pretty much done already, how long will it be before he follows me outside? How long before he accompanies me to the newsstand or to the grocer's? How long before he takes over my life? Think of the awkwardness, the embarrassment. He is not Harvey, after all; he's not invisible. And he certainly is not sweet natured or wise. And he's bigger than Harvey. Too big. I could swear he's growing.

I am thinking of phoning the ASPCA. Perhaps tomorrow, or the day after that. My bear is an unwanted animal, is he not? It is the business of the ASPCA, their duty, to take unwanted animals and treat them humanely. I would not want him hurt. Yes, I will definitely call the ASPCA by the end of the week, or early next at the latest, and tell them please to rid me of my bear, my beloved big white polar bear.

SHELLEY SAID, imagine what you know, or something like that, in his *Defence of Poetry*. Imagine what you know. The point implied is that there are different kinds of imagining. The first is to imagine what has never been. This is mere invention. Like the clock. Then, too, one may imagine an improvement on an existing situation. Makes a cloudy day sunny. But the best, most far-reaching use is to imagine what has been there all along, to dream into it as no one has ever dreamed, and to see what is there that never was so there. If one is inclined toward mere invention, one creates a Mr. Ed, a horse that talks. But if one uses the greater imagination, then that one, that Jonathan

Swift, comes up with the Houyhnhnm, talking horses that bear the burdens of civilization. Or perhaps bears that bear the burdens of civilization. Or Quasimodo, who bears civilization on his back.

So what am I getting at, you ask, as you stand in the archway, with your dangling ringlets, and a plate of sliced melons in your arms, and wearing that green and yellow sundress we bought you when we were in Puerto Rico way back when? I'm getting at you. Imagine that.

QUASIMODO, MY LAST DUCHESS, and the guy who left Miss Havisham at the altar went for a walk. Phew! said the guy who deserted Miss Havisham. That was a close call. But the truth is, I hadn't intended to run out on her, and had it not been for a broken carriage wheel detaining me that morning, I might have made it to the church on time. But man, am I grateful to that wheel! By the time I arrived, the now-famous Miss Havisham was three sheets to the wind and nutty as a fruitcake. Speaking of cake, did you get a load of that monstrosity? In any case, I got there four hours late. The guests had gone home. And she was still in her bridal gown, clearly bonkers. I watched from a safe distance, then took a powder. A few years later, I'd heard she'd had a baby. (Adopted? Right.) Mine, no doubt. Who else could have done it? So I went to the house to get a look at what my child had grown into, and she was as loony as her mother. A regular bitch. Funny thing is, I loved the Havisham dame once, especially when she was pregnant. She looked great, expecting.

I looked great, period, said the duchess, who refused to go last. And he had me killed because, according to him, I liked whatever I looked on and my looks went everywhere. The asshole duke. If he'd bothered to look at anything but the mirror, he would have seen that I only had eyes for him. But he didn't care. He was crazy with jealousy, baseless jealousy. When he had me pose for Fra Pandolf, I had no idea that the portrait would be the only thing left of me in the house. Had I only known that at the time, I would have fidgeted, prolonged the sitting. Now Ferrara calls my portrait a wonder. Asshole. If he had seen me, really seen who I was and how I worshipped him, he wouldn't have been so eager to hang me on the wall. Well, good luck to the next duchess is all I have to say.

And all I have to say, said Quasimodo, is, are you *kidding* me? I don't want to get all bent out of shape or anything. But will someone please tell me what is so goddam appealing about gypsies? I'm a *Frenchman,* for Chrissake. A *Frenchman.* Okay, I may not look like Maurice Chevalier, but I'm a hell of a lot smarter than that gypsy. And more sensitive. And heroic. And sweeter. Not to mention the fact that I'm strong as an ape, and can climb up a wall like one. Not to mention the fact that I was the prize resident of the greatest cathedral in Paris. They called me by my body. Why did they not call me by my soul? My devotion. And *she,* Esmeralda the bitch. Why could she not see past my appearance? Why could she not hear me when I whispered, *Je t'adore*? Instead, she gave her love to—I barely can speak the word—a *gypsy*. Gets my back up.

Sorry to hear about you and Janet. You and Janet seemed so right for . . . Oh, why do I say such a thing? You and Janet were wrong from the start. Anyone could see that a mile off. Oh, why do I say such a thing? Why do I say a word? What do I know about the inner workings of you and Janet? Or the outer workings, when it comes to that. You always seemed happy enough, I guess. But to tell the truth, I was pretty busy with some breakups of my own, with Lucille walking out on me barely a month after I walked out on Marlene. Nonetheless, you're my buddy, my best bud, so I want to find the words to comfort you at a time like this. She wasn't worth it. How's that? Or: You'll find someone else. Better? Or: Maybe you can work it out and get back together—you and Janine, that is, Janet.

The trouble with love . . .

Is there only one trouble?

The trouble with love is that it comes with hysteria, and it ought to be calm and under control.

But how is control possible, since love means delirium, passion? Didn't you just say something like that?

You confuse passion and love. Love requires the long steady view.

What if they cannot coexist, passion and the long steady view?

The long steady view is a kind of passion, only subdued. More pewter than silver.

That's just your rationalization, an excuse for not feeling passionate enough. I'll take passion over calm in love any day of the week.

Have it your way. But you should acknowledge what you're doing, deliberately opting for hysteria.

And how does one do that? Opt for hysteria.

LOVE REAL? GET REAL. Chemical weapons in Syria, that's real. Rows of kids' bodies not asleep. The killer of school children, the antigay thug, the drive-by shooter, the hit-and-run drunk. If they are real—and are they ever—love can't be real. And you can take that to the bank. The bank is real.

So now are you going to tell me about Saint Kevin in Ireland, on his knees, praying in his monk's cell that was so small he had to poke his right arm out the window? Along came a blackbird, which nestled in Kevin's outstretched hand, and laid a clutch of eggs. For days, weeks, Saint Kevin kept his arm outstretched until the eggs hatched. Then bye-bye blackbirds. A parable of love, of loving creatures great and small, including the lowlife blackbird. Remember, we're not talking about a robin or a lark or a bird that never wert (imagine that, Shelley). It was the ominous, creepy, cackling grackle for which Kevin gave his right arm. Kevin was for the birds. What about this story?

So now are you going to tell me about Saint Lucy in Rome, the highborn girl who strove to give her money to the poor? But her mother, Eutychia, wanted the dough for herself, and arranged an advantageous marriage for Lucy. To a pagan, if you please. Lucy was not pleased, and rebelled, the upshot depicted in later paintings of the saint, showing her holding a plate with a pair of eyes on it. Seems that soldiers tortured Lucy before knocking her off. They gouged out her eyes, or choked her until her eyes popped from their sockets. Yet the paintings show Lucy with her eyes intact, as well as the pair on the plate. If the tellers of the tale are to be believed, God restored sight to Saint Lucy—Lucy the light, the original four eyes, who died for her love of the poor.

Enough already. Who could possibly be taken in by such holy bunkum? How can love be real if its existence is illustrated by cock-and-bull stories of faith and martyrdom? Not real. Never real. Its crowning feature.

An earthenware pitcher of water, a plate of brown eggs, a geyser of blackbirds, a rock formation over a canyon simulating a bridge, you, good-byes in a Paris airport, an upright piano and the tinny echo of a damaged middle C as one knocks out "Someone to Watch Over Me," a gleaming wooden kayak tilting on wet rocks, you, a red cross on the top of an ambulance as seen from a roof in Athens, reruns of *Burns and Allen,* Blossom Dearie singing "I Walk a Little Faster," you, that green and yellow sundress, the puckered skin of a riverbed, the silence of a polar bear, flowers that come alive only at night, the awakening of orchids, a parade of Sikhs in full costume, reds and golds, a cracked jug in the corner of a cabin in Vermont, dusk light on the jug, a field bleached white by moonlight, the clamor of a keel on stones, you.

Who cares who sleeps with whom, except in those elevated love stories where everyone dies? The courtly loving Troilus and Cressida. Pyramus and Thisbe. Romeo and Juliet. That pair of nitwits in *Elvira Madigan,* who make such a to-do about their ill-fated affair, while Mozart diddles in the background. Tell you how I would have ended that movie. The two of them go into the forest for their suicide pact. We hear two gunshots. A moment passes, and one of them walks out. There ought to be a couple of ill-fated lovers called Sturm and Drang, whose whole story consists of shouting arias and tearing their hair out before leaping off a cliff. Bye-bye. Boo-hoo.

I'll take my lovers with a little more moxie, thanks. Hold the Mozart. Give me Frankie and Johnny. Or those kick-in-the-heads, Paul and Jack. Give me a dynamic duo called Fuck and Hugh, who refuse to knuckle under to familial pressure or social custom, and lived to tell about it. Or, if they don't live, at least they give life a shot. For my money, and that of most of the banks in Texas, the best couple in history was Bonnie and Clyde, who went down on each other for as long as possible, before they went down in flames.

The trouble with the exalted stories is that they're exalted. He's too good and she's too good. And when they run out of virtue, they kill themselves. Give me a break. Why do they care a plug nickel, whatever that is, about what others think? Oh dear. Oh dear. It's just too much. And the dumb-ass world that approves or disapproves doesn't give a shit anyway about who sleeps with whom. They just want to cluck about it. A chick I knew wasn't a widow three days before she went down for half the city of Hackensack. Did anybody call the cops?

Would you be an angel and unbuckle my belt, take down my pants, and suck my cock right here on Forty-second Street and Fifth? There's a good girl.

Mr. Schoefield, in love with solitude, built himself a cabin high on a hill in the northern Vermont woods. The year is 1849. For heat he chopped logs. For water he dug a well. For food he had berries, squirrels, rabbits, and the occasional duck. He did not read books. He did not play music. He neither sang nor hummed "I'll Go My Way by Myself," because it hadn't been written yet. He did not carve or whittle. He did not practice taxidermy or make ships in bottles. Memories of his family life back in Connecticut, he had a few at the beginning, but over the years the memories disappeared. Thoughts he had none, unless they involved the quotidian concerns of managing the cottage. An intruding fox or wildcat. Once in a while, a bear. When he took walks he paid only passive attention to the sights and sounds of the woods, neither collecting nor making note of plants or butterflies. In the summer he dealt with the heat. In the winter he dealt with the snow. That is, until the winter of 1851, when one afternoon, he was carrying an armful of logs from the woodpile to the cabin and heard two blasts from a double-barreled shotgun reverberating off the rocks studding a distant field. Then Mr. Schoefield collected his things and moved to Canada.

I read of a people who lived in a neglected corner of Africa, and all they ate was clay. No crops grew on their land, no grass or apple trees, or papayas. But lying in the soil there was plenty of moist red clay. So one day a man, weak from starvation, bent down and took the clay in his hands, and bit into it, and swallowed it. And the next day, a second man, having observed the first, did the same. And then a dozen men, women, and children followed suit. And then a thousand, until everyone in this neglected corner of Africa was eating clay for breakfast, lunch, and dinner, and for snacks. And though the people grew ill from the clay they ate, and many died very young, whenever someone would ask them—someone from a different place, where crops grew, and grass, and apple trees, and papayas—whenever such a person would ask why it was that they continued to eat clay, the people from this neglected corner of Africa would answer, often in unison: It's all we have.

It is to say, people will do anything if they are desperate enough. Or even if they aren't. People will do anything. The Buddhist monks who set themselves on fire in the public squares in Vietnam. The girl in my high school who bit off the pinky of another girl in a locker room brawl. The murderous savage at the Sandy Hook elementary school in Newtown, Connecticut. Syria. Weapons made from a chemistry set. My, my. Hard, hard. The open wounds of the world. And the choice: bandages or salt.

What was I looking for yesterday? Car keys? I don't think so. A cathedral town in Belgium—the name of it?

The name of Saint Kevin? Or Andreas Capellanus? Or the name of a Jesuit I knew at college? Good guy. Was I looking for his name? I doubt it. A shirt? A little-known fact about Mars? The minor chords in "Dancing in the Dark"? Every year, the eroding ice in the Arctic makes less of itself, so that eventually the world will be cold water, and the artists will have to create the polar bears from memory.

I stroll past the dead bushes and the stone-faced kids shouting obscenities at a woman in uniform. Oh, I remember now who I was looking for.

I HAVE NOT LOVED the world nor the world me—Byron, not Schoefield. Byron at his touchiest. I give to you and you give to me—nothing. Yet something insincere about this famous yawp. If the poet hadn't loved the world, why did he give a damn if the world loved him back? He would have omitted the second part of the line. Why would anyone in his right mind care if the world showed its love? That sort of display only turns your head, and gets you nowhere. Loving without expectations of reciprocity, on the other hand, well, that gets you everywhere. What's more: In the following stanza, Byron backs off, conceding a little here, a little more there, until he winds up hoping "goodness is no name, and happiness no dream."

But never mind all that. Isn't the world just too damn big to love? Unwieldy. Who could get his arms around the bloated bastard, with all its floods and quakes? Who could go for that? Better to love the world for its towpaths, weeds, and blackbirds. Your slightest look easily will unclose me—Cummings at his loveliest. Love the world not for its bigness, but rather for its slightest looks, its smallest gestures. A wave, for instance. I'm talking strangers waving to one another, hands raised briefly, making a fraction of an arc. On a towpath, say, past some weeds, beneath an umbrella of blackbirds. From your sullen arms I extract a wave.

One heart we have with poets. One memory of the world. One wish for the world. They forgive us everything.

"As when we come to love a thing for no better reason than that we have found it, and find it wants for love." He's on to something, Carl Phillips, though the sort of loving he names is not easy. The fact that someone or something wants for love says volumes. If you are not loved, by anyone, you may be sure that you are doing everything wrong with your life. You may have made yourself unworthy of love, objectively I mean, even hostile to love. That was Scrooge's principal flaw before his eleventh-hour conversion. He hated love. Come to think of it, his nephew loves him for no better reason than that Scrooge wanted for love. Would I have loved Scrooge?

Should I love you, whoever you are, simply because you are unlovable?

A man I knew a long time ago was unworthy of love, mine or anybody's. He reveled in the misfortunes of others, used what power he had to feed his dried-up little soul. I never heard him say a generous word about another human being. Not having seen him in years, I am happier for it. Still, once in a blue moon he comes to mind, always in a bad light. It disturbs me to remember him, and his lies, and gossip, and treachery, and cowardice. I think I'll love him, for the hell of it.

OH, HELL. I'll include my ailments, too. Why not? They're family. And not just my family, either. If you think of the entire history of human experience gathering in everyone's body—the basic genetic code passed down through thousands of generations, millions of years—then our ailments and infirmities are as much a part of us as our healthy organs.

Love me, love my shoulder operation to tighten ligaments stretched out of shape in a basketball game, in my twenties. Love my two lower back operations for slipped discs that refused to slip back into place in my thirties. Love my missing thyroid gland and its synthetic replacement. Love my prostate cancer, radiated out of existence.

Love one-fifth of my face below my right eye, which was removed to dig out a melanoma, and then put back. My plastic surgeon told me, "Roger, you've had all the discomfort of a face-lift, and none of the benefits."

With these residents of my body controlled or under control, you'll forgive me, doctor, if I cancel Tuesday's appointment for a checkup. At this stage, I'm content to live with what I've got. I've got the sun in the morning, and a couple of dead nerves from the second back operation keeping me awake at night. But it's all good. These ailments are mine, part of me, nearly all of me. So why not take all of me. Come to think of it, doc. I'm canceling all my future appointments, not just Tuesday. And if my PSA creeps up a bit, and you discover another rhomboid-shaped brown stain on my face, the odds are that all my diseases will outlive me anyway.

After I'm gone, where will my ailments go? To others, I suppose, as the species continues to accumulate features of its own frail evolution. Getting this, getting rid of that. My miserable body contains the history of the race, baby. I can't give it anything but love.

Like a patient convalescing from a long disease, Esther leans on the bannister as she descends the stairs, and watches Michael walk toward the front door. He does not turn back to look at her. He is filled with anticipation of his new life, his new chapter, as he puts it, on his journey, as he puts it. He's only just begun to live, as he puts it. He has forgotten that he ever loved Esther. And Esther? Well, she is the old life. Thirty-two years of the old life. Out on the street, he quickens his step, his shoes clicking like a revolver misfiring on an empty chamber.

Now Esther is alone with the choice: to obliterate Michael from her thoughts and love him no more, or to continue to love him in his absence. She chooses the latter. And whenever one of her friends will deride him in front of her, she will protest, and will mention his good points. And when pressed as to why she does this time and time again, when she knows perfectly well that Michael is a shit, Esther will reply that she'd rather be lonely than happy with somebody else, and that as long as she loves Michael, nothing will have changed. And nothing has.

People sometimes get married for the same reasons poets sometimes write sonnets. Form rescues content.

O. Blushing Bride, daughter of Mr. and Mrs. Parents of the Bride, of Whocares, Rhode Island, and Breathless, South Carolina, was married yesterday to Handsome Groom III, son of Mr. Father of the Groom, of Boston and Maine, and Mrs. Mother of the Groom, of Baltimore and Ohio. The ceremony was performed in No Standards Church by the rector, Canon Dearly Beloved. Miss Sister was the maid of honor; Mr. Brother, the best man. The bride, who made her debut at the Desperado Cotillion, is an alumna of Small College. The bridegroom, a graduate of Large Eastern University, is with Substantial National Bank. The couple will reside in Bestchester.

Or so it reads.

Yet now he rails at her for thinking Vermeer was a Yiddish expression. And she throws a raving fit in Costco, of all places, because he waltzed in late tonight and spilled rye on the Cuisinart. He hums "Love Me or Leave Me." She hums "Here's That Rainy Day." He picks up the latest *Oui*.

That, of course, comes long after the stripping of the wallpaper, the staining of the floors, the exposure of the beams. *When those beams are exposed, we're going to have some joint here, baby, I'll tell you that. Look at those beams. Did you ever see such beams?*

Of the six marriages announced on page eighty-three of the Sunday paper, 2.2 will fail, 2.3 will last, 1.5 will fail and last. The lovely faces fill their squares; young women with clear, glinting eyes and miraculous teeth. *Miraculous, nothing! Cost us a mint to get those teeth in line! When she was twelve, we thought she'd wind up marrying Bugs Bunny! Ha-ha.* Ah, Mr. Wedding Photographer, you catch them in the pink. These are action shots, are they not? The ball at the crack of the bat; the sail blown full; the trout in a pirouette, all splash and color. You sports photographer, you.

The truth is that Blushing's folks did not, when it comes down to it, really "announce" the engagement of their daughter. They could barely spit out the words, so dismayed were they that their little princess should throw herself away on a wimp like Groom. The truth is that Handsome's dad said the boy was marrying beneath him. The truth is that Sister is sick with envy, and Brother red with hate. The truth is that no one thinks it will work.

Do you, Blushing?

I do.

Do you, Handsome?

Oh, very much.

Go to it anyway, Bride and Groom. Damn the statistics. Full speed, deliberate speed. Strip that wallpaper, expose those beams, expose those hearts. Take this waltz. There is no good reason on earth why you should reside happily ever after. At the same time, there is no good reason you should *not*. And if the truth is that your goose is cooked at the altar, then the truth can be made wrong, too, you know, can be made to look like a dope in a single, spur-of-the-moment decision to be gentle and patient—against the jeering mobs and the hoots outside. Are you game or "Just Married"?

In the morning, in the Plaza, the two of them in bed prop up their iPads against their knees and address the wedding pictures. Between the melon and the sweet rolls, they agree they both photograph exquisitely.

On the other hand: Good evening. We are gathered on this beautiful beach, as friends and family of Genevieve and Max, to witness and celebrate their marriage. My name is Roger. Genevieve was my writing student. She turned out well, nevertheless. I am happy to be a friend to both these wonderful people. Recklessly, they have asked me to officiate at this ceremony, though I have no official title or authority to do so. For this, I apologize to you all, and for those who believe in God, to God.

At this time, Genevieve and Max would like to thank everyone for being here at this celebration. To their many friends, they are forever grateful. To their parents—Carol and Phil and Michael and Laura—they thank you for the sacrifices you have made, for the unqualified love you have shown them, and for the lives you have opened for them, and inspired. One feels the special presence of Phil Crane this evening, who would be so proud of his daughter and so pleased about the man with whom she is about to spend her life.

Max and Genevieve met at Oxford, in a study-abroad program offered by UMass Amherst. Upon seeing Genevieve, Max asked [quote], "Do I know you from somewhere?" Genevieve dismissed his approach as a lame pickup line, but it turned out to be true. The two of them had lived two floors apart in the same freshman dorm.

As boring as this anecdote is, it illustrates a difference between Max and Genevieve. I learned the story when I asked each of them to answer a number of questions about their life and ideas. Well, I can't say that there were a lot of ideas. But they each described their how-did-you-meet event characteristically. Max wrote a dutiful, straightforward businessman's paragraph relying on the facts. The writer Genevieve wrote about Max's blue eyes, and of feeling [quote], "There is too much handsomeness here." In answer to other questions, Max noted how kind and caring Genevieve is. Genevieve cited Max's self-confidence, his deadpan humor, and his terrific sense of judgment. Also his love of baseball. [To him] Which team, Max? [He says, the Red Sox.] So much for judgment. Max is a neat freak. Genevieve has the habit of losing her phone, wallet, and keys. Still, Max takes comfort in the apparent chaos of the universe. They both take comfort in each other. And they give comfort to their friends, young and old. It's comforting to see how solid these two good people are together.

Genevieve and Max: People often think love's simple because it arises naturally, in one's nature. But love is no simpler than nature is simple. It makes demands. It requires corresponding actions. It takes concentration, patience, trust. It asks for attentiveness and creative listening. For a will toward understanding. For a willingness to

So at last it has come to this. Since marriage requires a leap of faith, it is time to leap. [Take rings from Michael (father) and Eddy (best man). Give them to Max and Genevieve.]

Max, do you take Genevieve to be your wedded wife, to have and to hold from this day forward, for better, for worse, for richer, for poorer, in sickness and in health, to love and to cherish, until death parts you? [Max: I do.]

Genevieve, do you take Max to be your wedded husband, to have and to hold from this day forward, for better, for worse, for richer, for poorer, in sickness and in health, to love and to cherish, until death parts you? [Genevieve: I do.]

Kiss away, kids. Ladies and gentlemen: the perfectly married, Genevieve and Max.

On the other hand: This is a hearing test.

Can you hear this?

Sounds like church bells, people laughing, glasses clinking.

Can you hear this?

Is it, "Our Love Is Here to Stay"?

Can you hear this?

What? The baby's cry? Yes, I can hear it.

Can you hear this?

A door slamming, I think. And china breaking.

Can you hear this?

It's faint. I can barely make it out. It sounds like the wearing away of the inside of a tunnel or a universal joint or maybe the melting underside of ice on a frozen pond. Something eroding out of sight, from the area one cannot see. But I can't be certain.

Very good. That's exactly what it was.

BECAUSE YOU DID NOT LOOK for riches, which was lucky because there were no riches to be had; or station in society, because the only station available was a whistle-stop; or stature, or ambition for stature, or ambition for anything, because no ladder presented itself, nothing to climb. Or safety, you did not even look for that, though one would think that safety would be one of the basics. But you did not look for safety. Or mirrors. You certainly did not look for mirrors. (You're so not vain.)

Fact is, I cannot recall you looking for anything, or requiring anything, much less making demands for anything. The carpenter knows what he's about. Same goes for the Toyota repairman, and the tinker with the wheel that whets the knives. Same goes for you, unseeking, impassive, needing nothing superfluous, including sunflowers or chocolates. Emeralds did not enter your calculus. It was all quite simple, really. The beauty of water basins, the trace of an eclipse, sardines blazing their silver boulevards in the teeth of the sea. Wooden steps to the beach, me at the piano. That was plenty, you said. Because all you wanted was here and now. I gave you here and now. Tell the judges that.

I LOVE YOU the gray way the creek looks in a light rain. I love you the brown way of that anomalous tree, the wavy one between the taller pines, in our backyard. I love you the luscious way a plum tastes on an afternoon when one sees a plum on a plate and unconsciously grabs it. I love you the frail, sure way of daisies, the shiny kettle way of French press coffee, the breezy way of September, the resigned, determined way of "September Song." And the touching way of a dog's face, I love you that way, too. And the moth beating its wings on the window way. And the anticipatory way of a conversation, when the one you're with is about to tell you something new about the etymology of a familiar word, or an idiom like "the devil and the deep blue sea," or about themselves. I love you that way as well. I love you the way one changes one's mind about having dessert, the way a bus has a hissy fit before a stop, the way you tie a bandage on your finger, or on mine, the way a book falls open to a reference about Chaucer. I love you the way horses snort, ducks bat their wings, the way e. e. cummings loves, the way Doris Day sings "It's Magic," the way Baby Boomers go gooey at a James Taylor concert outdoors, on a lawn. I love you that way and this, hair up or down, sneakered or well-heeled, shouting or sleeping, tired or more tired, the way you look tonight or any night. How do I love thee?

Love is wonderful the seventh time around, he had crooned to her at their wedding in the presence of a few friends, alluding to the fact that for him it was his third marriage, and for her, the fourth. Everyone had laughed, cheered, and clinked glasses. Now, their guests had departed and they are seated at one of the linen-covered tables on the lawn, sipping cabernet and chillin', as the kids say. It is September, and the clear air has an edge to it. A nearby pond ripples a bit nervously. The trees swing their skirts in the wind. He raises his glass to her, she to him.

Not a word passes between them, as if these two are perched atop history itself. And what is there to say, anyway? They are about to embrace the surprise of a marriage of no surprises. Dull, you think. Yet in their midsixties, the idea of surprise isn't nearly as attractive as anticipation, just as in the great works of literature, the classics, anticipation trumps surprise to deepen the emotions involved. You wouldn't wish to be surprised by what happened to Troilus and Cressida. You wouldn't wish to be shocked at a turnabout for Lear. You would not want to be staring at a point on the ocean's horizon over which the sun was expected to rise, only to see the moon rise there instead. You would want the sun to come up, just as it has for millions of years, affording you the quiet appreciation of the universe, as well as the delusion that you were in control of it. That is what you would want.

Similarly, these two people sit wordless at the table, anticipating the sunrise in each other, and smile out loud.

THE PEOPLE WHO FIRST DISCOVERED LOVE were made of bark and Kleenex, and they lived in a trolley car far far away. They handled hazardous materials. When the security guards were drunk or asleep, the love discoverers would play with live electrical wires or walk barefoot on the wall of the reservoir that once was the New York Public Library, singing their hearts out, as if they didn't have a care in the world. In fact, they didn't. They sang "Something Makes the World Go Round." They sang "I Want to Be Something by You." They sang "What Is This Thing Called . . ." But they had no word for the missing word. Some liked blueberries, others fried chicken. They did not watch their weight, and no one else did either. Around them, and over and under as well, hard-boiled eggs were blown this way and that, but mainly this. And in the evenings, when big glasses of milk were served with Oreo cookies with double-size fillings, and the three-piece band of songbirds showed up in tuxes, to brighten their lives, the discoverers of love would sing appreciation songs or affection songs, and reminisce about the long ago and the times they took their favorite girls (or boys, as it were) to the all-day cartoons, and bought them corsages of jelly apples, and stole a kiss that they would never return.

One, it was said, was tall. And so was another. He wore a harness and a breastplate made of shale. When finally he proposed marriage, his heart was in his mouth, which made it difficult for him to speak, as he was about to make his momentous discovery. So he said nothing. Instead, he took his girl by the shoulders, looked into her eyes, found kindness there, and loved.

How do you know? I thought, but failed to ask the professor after his lecture. The program called for Q&A. The professor answered questions about his life and upbringing, his work in science and in ecology specifically. His talk sailed way over my head. But at one point he'd said that we must love the natural world, even though the natural world does not love us. Our love goes unrequited, said the professor. Nature does not show its love. Birds, bees, even educated fleas don't do it. And I thought, how do you know?

When the creek is still, and the pitch pines and tupelo trees around it, still, and even the hectic killifish still, for a moment at least, and the shiners and the snappers and the dragonflies and damselflies, having alighted on the dark wet stones, can easily be mistaken for dead; when the ducks hesitate, and their down is unruffled by the wind, and the osprey and the purple martins are quiet as mice, which are also still; when there is no wind, and the horseshoe crabs don't lift a finger, and the mosquitoes, too, even they, still as the speckles on a motionless snake—when all this occurs, or does not occur, but is, how can one know that in its stillness, nature is not taking us in, meditating upon our being, and loving us in its impenetrable way?

But nature does not show its love, you say. And I say, how better to show it than by being—not certain, of course, if this speculation of mine is mere mind play, yet hoping it is not. Birds in their freedom, beasts, too. White oaks as well. Also trout.

Life loves. Love life. Driving on the highway, I am stuck behind a delivery truck from East Coast Custom Car. On the back of the truck, in bright yellow lettering is a list of things sold at East Coast Custom Car: stereos, alarm systems, bed liners, 4x4 accessories, trailer hitches, fog lights, wheels, "and so much more." I make a note to include these items in my accounts, then turn off toward the bay, which is winter blue already. The powerboats have disappeared. The cormorants swarm in a black mass near the mouth of a creek, their snakeheads craning for invisible killifish. I watch for a while, slip in a CD of André Previn playing "The Second Time Around" and add these things to my list as well.

Then I drive home, where I make more entries still. In the mail are new pictures of the grandchildren taken by Ginny, who is away visiting them. I share a dish of cold mashed potatoes with the dog; the wind kicks up; the fat pine on the front lawn struts in place in the late afternoon; shadows smudge the hedges; day hook-slides into night. I think of high school baseball, then basketball. The Spaldeen moon hangs so low, it looks as if it is about to fall to earth and bounce.

This inventory is getting out of hand. Last week alone I made more than a thousand new entries, and I never erase the old ones. If this keeps up, I will require a dozen ledgers, and even then my accounts will be woefully incomplete. Every year it is the same. I prepare my inventory for Thanksgiving, to say grace, and always come up short.

In a different season, W. D. Snodgrass wrote "April Inventory," an ambling elegiac list consisting mostly of the things he had gladly failed at. His poem ends on the lines "There is a loveliness exists, / Preserves us, not for specialists." Specialists were the target of his complaint. The successful people around him had zeroed in on particular and limited interests and had been rewarded for the categories they had made of their lives, while he, in unsuccessful contrast, had flopped about and picked up a few scattered items of value, like loveliness and the ability to love. My inventory is sort of like that. It is a record of haphazard events, the serendipity that Jane Jacobs used to say made for a pleasant city. So I jot down the stuff I bump into, or that bumps into me—life's precious accidents good and bad, ridiculous, astonishing. The task is overwhelming.

Did you know that there is a species of turtles called Kemp's ridley, which are born on a nesting beach in Mexico (only a few survive the hungry bird attacks) and then swim madly out to sea, where they are carried by the Gulf Stream all the way up to Long Island, New York (it takes three to five years), where they feed for a year on the defenseless spider crab as a training exercise before they take off again and swim down to the Chesapeake Bay area in Maryland, where they eat the much tougher blue claw crab for which the Long Island boot camp has prepared them? Needless to say, they made my inventory. As did the deer, the full-size antlered stag I saw the other day at dusk, as I was walking down the main street of our village. He stepped out of a driveway, as if he'd stepped out of a dream, looked about to panic, saw it was only me and trotted, head high, down the center of the street.

Lives this month: two new young friends get married on the beach. Two brave old friends fight cancer. Another attempts to resist a deteriorating muscle disorder. Deaths this month: the philosopher Isaiah Berlin; Victor Mills, the father of the disposable diaper; and Francine Katzenbogen, a lottery winner who lavished her millions on her many beloved cats. Miss Katzenbogen died of an asthma condition severely aggravated by her cats. Cross reference: Katzenbogen/cats.

The moon is sky-high now, a small pale eye at the top of the dark. A light plane blinks by overhead. A letter from a friend, a photographer, whose child is gravely ill. He includes a picture of the boy. In a corner is the photographer's shadow, like spilled ink. Too many loved ones in distress this Thanksgiving, too many entries of that sort. In adversity they conduct themselves like soldiers. A sleepless night. A new day full of migrating ducks and edible smells from the kitchen. I am ill-prepared again, but I give it a shot.

Thank you for this sublime mess. For human courage and for turtle courage. For newlyweds, cormorants, philosophers, photographers, Miss Katzenbogen, André Previn, disposable diapers, moons, dogs, deer, trailer hitches, fog lights, wheels, and so much more.

The shadow of the one who took the photograph sometimes appears in the photograph, and is said to spoil it. I can't see why. If anything, the shadow offers substance to the scene, as if God himself were captured

Give my love to the substance and to the shadow, and to the smoked salmon. And to the bagel. Don't forget the bagel. Give my love to Quasimodo, my last duchess, Mr. Havisham, and to Don Quixote and Wile E. Coyote and Peter Lorre and Sydney Greenstreet and Broadway. Give my love, not merely my regards, to Broadway. And to Ezio Pinza singing "Some Enchanted Evening." Give my love to the 1969–1970 Knicks, and to the 1955 Yanks, also 1961, and to Jackie Robinson. To Bette Davis, too. And to her eyes. Give my love to Bette Davis, and Sammy Davis Jr., and Harry Connick Jr., and Absorbine Jr., and Junior Gilliam. Oh, and how could I forget Jeanette MacDonald? Give my super-dooper love to Jeanette MacDonald, whose singing voice was so pleasantly distracting, you nearly forgot she was a babe. I mean hot. *Rose Marie*? "Indian Love Call"? Give my love to swimming in the health club pool, and in the ocean, and to one good thwacking forehand, and the very occasional three-pointer (at my age!). Look at Dad! Give my love to "Look at Dad!" To the musty library, to the piano bar, to Madison Avenue on a blazing autumn afternoon, to a long long winding road in Vermont, a letter from a long-lost friend, to friends in general, but not to generals. Give it to J. M. Synge, Yeats (both Jack and William B.), Wordsworth, Shelley and his imaginative imagination, Donne, Marvell, Thomas Gray, and Eliot (George not T. S.). And Marianne Moore, and her apteryx-awl. And Jimmy Baldwin. Give lots of love to Jimmy Baldwin. Give my love to Israel, Italy, and

Ireland, the three eyes of the world. Give my love to the Marlboros (haven't seen them since my twenties), and to the Jamesons, neat, and to Bonnie and Clyde, messy. And to the four eyes of Saint Lucy. And to Brooks Brothers and the Marx Brothers and the Gershwin brothers, also to Joyce Brothers. Why not? Give my love to new cars, old Scotch, tall trees, short stories, big breaks, small potatoes, sweet corn, sour grapes and sourpusses, to thick thieves and Slim Pickens, wild strawberries, tame shrews, etc. etc., et al. et al. Give my love to etc. and et al. To the whole shebang, now that you mention it, the megillah, the enchilada, the beandendalls, the ups and downs, ins and outs, the jots and tittles. And to Y. A. Tittle, too. And give my love to you. Did you think I forgot? To the east, west, north, and the south of you. Especially the south of you.

CARTOON IN *The New Yorker* many years ago. An Indian sitting in a teepee, summoning his woman: "You come, when I'm calling you hoo hoo hoo, hoo hoo hoo."

IF I SHOULD FALL ASLEEP in my chair and not awaken (you get my drift), would you be good enough to reserve a seat for me at an outdoor restaurant (the one on Madison in the Sixties will do), so that I may look out on a world I've so admired (abhorred, whatever) and occasionally see something interesting? A woman on her way to a dance hall to meet a man she does not know. A couple in their sixties returning from their wedding, holding hands. Two black guys in identical powder blue pullovers, walking with their arms around each other's shoulders. An anxious man in conversation with a bear.

By nightfall, the scene before the restaurant will have changed, and the street population diminished to the point where there are but two people remaining, one on either corner. On the corner to my left, a young man will crouch like a bowler in an alley and roll an orange down the sidewalk until it stops at the feet of the other person on the street, on the corner to my right, who picks up the orange, and examines it in all its orangeness. That person would be you.

The Greeks had it that the illuminations of the world derive from rays our eyes project. More Hellenistic drivel. Yet sometimes, in my bleak tunnels, when the floods descend, and darkness, real or imagined, seeps into my foul soul, dripping like black paint on a black door, you will look my way, and I am illuminated.

At 3:35 on an October afternoon in 2012, Professor Kronenberger addresses his variorum edition in progress of the early poetry of John Skelton, as he always does at this hour, and pores over the pages. He has been working on this project since 1988, and has high hopes of completing volume one of a projected six volumes by the fall of 2019. If they asked him, he could write a book, but at his own speed and in his own good time. Of course, no one has asked him. So engrossed is he with his labor of love, he has not paid attention to the TV reports of an oncoming storm. How could he? He doesn't own a TV. And since he lives alone with almost no contact with the world outside his little two-story cottage, he has had no one to warn him to evacuate. At 4:14, Superstorm Sandy hits Staten Island, where Professor Kronenberger has lived for fifty-three years. His parents, Mildred and Otto, who died last March within two weeks of each other, both from pneumonia, bequeathed him the place, and though he misses his parents from time to time, he has to confess that with the two of them gone, he has that much more space for his Skelton material. So in love is Professor Kronenberger with his project that at 5:07 he fails to notice the tide, lifted by Superstorm Sandy, creeping toward his house. At 5:48, it reaches his basement. At 6:09 the first floor. At 7:51, water rises to the second floor, where Professor Kronenberger is now proofreading his footnotes on the distinction between Skeltonics and macaronics. By 8:57, the rising water has ripped his house from its pilings, and is floating it on the street that leads to the sea. At 11:00 on the

I FELL IN LOVE WITH YOU the first time I looked into them there peepers. Jeepers. That's how it works sometimes. Something or someone catches your attention and you are consumed with affection and sympathy. Then time passes. You write (compose or paint), and what is left of love is art, a kind of ongoing love. All that's left of Van Gogh's stunned potato eaters is the painting. Of the War of 1812, Tchaikovsky's overture. *Vita brevis,* but of Robert Capa the photograph of a rebel Spanish soldier shot dead, living forever. (Strange shadows in that picture, too.)

From misery, art builds studios. From want, choirs. Watch me. I go to the town dump to glean a fender from a fender bender, also a blender. Let's hear it for the mess—the twisted door of a van, posts from awnings, horseshoes—and for the impression that I may make something beautiful of it all. Such a prideful notion. Why does it occur to me? Why does a city fire escape in the summertime strike me as beautiful? Why did the inmates of the mental hospital in Beirut strike me as beautiful? The children flailing about in their own excrement. The legless woman scuffling toward me like the Frankenstein monster, because she needed to tell me that nothing was wrong with her. Why did the Frankenstein monster strike Mary Shelley as beautiful, odious and beautiful? A karaoke box. A plastic figure of Neptune with a broken trident.

It's what art is. No? Detritus transformed by love into something sacred? We live in moments of surprise at our own beauty, the celebration of accidents. The blessings of accidents. And comes the night when Superduperstorm Sandy the Second devours the northeastern states, and floods away every scholar's house, every farm, every van and awning, every horse, and lifts every body of water into oblivion, what will remain of us? A song.

No thanks. I think I'll stay out here in the rainstorm, on the rocks or the damp sand, where I can calculate the shelves of the sea, and traipse about the unmapped territory of what has come to be known as our relationship. You know how characters in the better plays do not really talk to each other, but rather past each other, addressing some abstract listener who resembles themselves, except for the stare—how they do not care if anyone actually hears what they say? That's us. Nothing surprises me anymore, or you anymore, for that matter. These endless conversations that wind up in the tar pits. Out in my kayak the other morning, I passed a pair of egrets who had staked out the bow of a Boston Whaler and stood there and beheld the creek, without acknowledging each other. Either they were so familiar with each other that they did not need to assure themselves of the other's presence. Or they knew that they were bound by tradition to stand together with nothing between them but the wobbly boat they stood on. That's us.

I walk a mile or so down the beach. The sea goes black. The sky goes white. A tern, I think, patrols the vague horizon. The Kemp's ridley turtles take off for Mexico. Before the year is out, I'll leave this spot. Raindrops cling to the tips of the sea grass. I become their disciple. I have no idea where you are, or you, I.

You could not believe I would say such a thing. I could not believe you would say such a thing. Such a thing. No Indian giver can take it back—that cat, that bag. Exposed to the light, it seems, if anything, more not less monstrous, those things we said, like a big something that should not be big—a giant wren, for instance, a dandelion one hectare in circumference. Anything that size becomes horrific. Even rabbits. Even Harvey. You want to run for the exits. I know I do. But the exits were soldered shut in the 1950s, and cell phones are yet to be invented. I've always wondered what it would be like to crash my car, and the air bag never stops expanding, and I can hear my ribs crack from the pressure, one by one, until all the air in the world is in that bag, and none in me, and then I cave, a slack bellows.

The intervention of facts:

She says: The first known bird is the archaeopteryx.

He says: The Chinese invented the clock.

She says: Larry Doby was the second Negro League player to make it to the majors.

He says: Guyla is a town on the White Koros River near the Romanian border.

She says: Nina Simone sang "Spring Is Here."

He says: It was Jeanette MacDonald.

She says: I paid the AmEx bill in time.

He says: AmEx says you didn't, and there's going to be a late charge.

She says: They are in error.

He says: There will be penalties.

She says: Fine.

He says: Fine. And flushed with anger, goes to the bookshelf to take down the *Encyclopedia of Baseball.*

As to the Chinese and their clock: Are you telling me there was no one, not a single peasant in China, in all of China for Chrissake, who did not forget that his people invented the clock? Including the inventor? Give me a break. We forget who we are. The Germans, the Japanese, the Cambodians, the English, the Italians, the people of Rwanda, of Uganda, ourselves from time to time. A cynic might say that our murderous spasms occur when we remember who we are. Really are. I don't believe it.

Weird, I say. The emperor studies the new French

contraption in his hands, and sings: "I didn't know what time it was. Then I met you." In Chinese, of course.

NATURALLY, HE DISMISSED IT as "neglect," and it *was* neglect—the absence of attention, the omission of attention—as when a town in which an industry once thrived (a steel mill or a shoe factory) is fallen from neglect, and the eaves of the roofs sag soaked with rain, and the door of the bank vault lies open to houseflies, the grocer's shelves are thick with dust, the druggist's shelves the same; and nothing remains of the schoolyard except a jungle gym in a heap of pipes and a chain-link fence that has been yanked from its stanchions. Still, he was right. Technically, it was neglect. Why give it a moment's thought?

Of course, if he *had*—given it a moment's thought, that is—he might not have made that lame joke about Van Gogh's ear. He might not have forgotten to remember that their song was "Evergreen," when he sat down to play "The Way We Were" instead. But he didn't think. Just like him. This happens to him more often than it should. Then he concludes, clinically: Life's like this—a perpetual pursuit of small satisfactions such as being funny, or being charming, or being anything. Nickel-and-dime decisions, yet oh my, the repercussions. Chaos without the theory.

I wish I could tell him how to stop. But frankly, the consequences of one's little stumbles get so tumultuous sometimes that one's amazement at them overtakes the desire for self-improvement. So he goes on as before. An ice storm comes to mind. The interesting thing about an ice storm is that it isn't defined until it's over. Then you see the ice.

I'll work nights. Oh. That's right. I already do work nights. Okay. I'll wash floors. How's that? I'll wash ceilings, too. I'll scrub chandeliers. I'll enlist in the marines, invade Syria, establish Chemistry for Peace, where Christians, Muslims, and Jews, too, work together for a brighter Syria. What do you think of that? I'll go deep-sea diving, deeper than anyone ever has, deeper than Sylvia Earle, who is known as Her Deepness—deeper than Sylvia—where I'll swim, with all sorts of dangerous and colorful fishes, and discover treasure from Spanish galleons, including gold doubloons and pieces of eight, pieces of nine, if that's what you want. I'll train for Cirque du Soleil or Lord of the Dance, so that you'll have the chance of watching me step dance to an Irish jig, or juggle a dozen milk bottles as I zip along a zip line strung between the Brooklyn and Manhattan bridges, thus offering you the choice of a jig or a juggle. Or, if it's the more intellectual life that impresses you, I shall get my PhD in astrophysics, and learn many astrophysical things. I'll discover a galaxy. I'll name a new planet. I'll de-name an old planet. What exactly do you want? No. Forget I said that. I do not wish to seem uncooperative. Tell you what: I'll recite *Moby-Dick*. I'll finish *The Magic Mountain*. No one ever finishes *The Magic Mountain*. But I will. I'll do it for you. I'll hold my breath for six minutes. Make that eight. I'll hold my breath for ten minutes, while singing "I'd cry for you, die for you" with my lips closed, and walk a mile for a Camel and smoke it and drink a glass of water at the same time. You can tell I'm running out of ideas. Here's what I'll do. I'll jog around our house, around and around, faster and faster, breaking into a canter, a gallop, until I wear a circular depression in the land, deeper and deeper, and the house perches on a tall funnel of earth, maybe three hundred feet high. And then I'll fill the ditch around the house with water, and I'll build a drawbridge attached by chains to the house, which may be raised or lowered, to admit visitors or not. But I shall be your only visitor, and when I cross the moat, I shall dynamite the drawbridge behind me, so that you will be trapped in your house, with me. Then, I shall approach you as you perch on your red velvet cushion, and ask, as politely as I am able, What do you want of me?

Tyler hits the road after a knock-down-drag-out fight with Ali, in which he stood at the foot of the bed and told her he never loved her. She knew it was true, because she never loved him, either. Nobody loves anybody, she thought, she always thought. People stay together, part, opt for hysteria, take pictures of shadows, swim over and under each other, or go to Applebee's and fall for Tracey with the boobs, or have small groups over to the house, or buy flowers or wallets, or flirt with Gus or Katey at the cookout, then die. But nobody loves anybody. It's just something to say.

Where will I go this time? Tyler wonders. Terre Haute? Akron? Akron. He remembers a really neat runners shop there, near another Applebee's with a waitress called Tam. He rents a basement apartment in a dentist's office on the main drag, with an Acura rusting in the back. He buys a flat-screen TV, on which he watches fishing shows and shows that sell jewelry and household appliances. He also joins a support group for people with the cancer, though he doesn't have the cancer. Or maybe he does.

Ali joins the volunteer fire department. Stronger than many of the men, she learns how to wield a hose, and steer the yellow truck. She studies the history of fire departments and learns that they began in ancient Rome, where they were private businesses. If some Roman's house caught fire, a chariot or some other conveyance would bring buckets of water to the site and then the guy who owned the equipment would negotiate a price with the guy whose house was on fire, before putting it out. If they didn't reach a deal, the house burned to the ground. Ali studies more, about the Great London Fire and the Triangle Shirtwaist Factory fire in New York. She strikes up an affair with the fire chief, Chad. During sex, also before and after, neither party speaks.

When Tyler and Ali get back together eight months later, he tells her he always loved her, and she tells him the same. They live much as they had before Tyler left, except that Ali maintains her interest in the history of fire departments, and Tyler joins a support group for people with gambling addictions. The meetings are held in the nearby Lutheran church, and are attended by a striking brunette named Angelica. They are invited to join Chad and his wife, Mindy, for Lobster Night at TGI Friday's. During dessert, over strawberry sundaes, Mindy reveals that she has joined a club devoted to the apocalypse, and Tyler is interested in this. She tells Ali and Tyler that the world will end sometime around Christmas.

Here, at the edge of a cliff in Jersey, I picture you, the spitting image of Generalissimo Franco, prancing around in your shiny black riding boots, and then haranguing the masses from your bulletproof balcony at the Palace of Blasts and Noise, or whatever it was called. Of course, you are younger and prettier than Franco, and female, and alive. But that's what comes to mind. When I think of those years together that were so crowded with shouting in various languages, small wonder we had little time for lovemaking. Hate-making choked the calendar. At the end of the day, I was hoarse, while you, astride your horse and apparently indefatigable, rode off to whip the servants. This can't be love, I thought. If that was love, I'll take war.

Still, I never felt the need of a summit of peaceniks, disposed to tell us how to work out our differences. How like the dead you lay, save for the sweet sputterings of your lips. Our borders touched, while throughout the night, troops manned the tanks and rolled cannon into position within range of our contiguous hearts.

Even if you're not Generalissimo Franco, I cannot help but notice that you're much too much, and much too very very. I take it back. You're not even very. What ever possessed me to say such a thing? If I say very, you know I don't mean it. If I say very very, you know I don't mean it twice. Why would one need to say, I love you very much? What's wrong with a simple, I love you? If you loved me half as much as I love you, you'd never say *very*, which suggests less than half of half as much. You're much too very very to ever be in Webster's dictionary? First of all, you aren't in Webster's dictionary, neither is *very very*, and, now that I think of it, Webster ought to take out *very*, too. If Webster can be wrong about the "lion's share," well, what's next? Get rid of *very*. No one would miss it much.

And I'm absolutely right? Why do I need to be absolutely right? I don't need "absolutely." Right?

Which brings me to the pale moon, which does not excite me. It's Jeter up with the bases loaded in the bottom of the ninth, and the Yanks down two: that excites me. Or it's a murder, with Holmes, Spade, or Philo Vance on the case. Or it's an oversize dish of soft chocolate and vanilla ice cream, swirled. Or an airtight sentence, where not one word is unnecessary or out of order. The American Constitution. That excites me. But the pale moon? Oh, yes. The nearness of you. That does excite me. And it also thrills and delights me.

Of course, the nearness of you to me implies the nearness of me to you, and I have no idea if that excites you. I have no idea what excites you. Well, some small idea. George Clooney and Johnny Depp excite you, you've made that clear. And shoe stores, they get you all stirred up as well. Beaches, puppies, you've mentioned them. For all I know, it's the pale moon that excites you. What, may I ask, is so fucking exciting about the pale moon?

AND AS LONG AS we're on the language of love, I just want to say, I think you're awesome. Awesome. I mean it. In every way, *awesome*. Me? I'm awesome, too? Seriously? Because if you do—think I'm awesome, I mean—that would be well, you know. What I'm saying is that if you thought I was awesome, and I thought the same of you, so that we ascertained a similar mutual feeling, that is, we made the same equivalent assessment of each other's worth, with neither one of us feeling either superior or inferior to the other, in terms of the intensity of our attitudes, each of us secure in the knowledge that we were experiencing the same emotions concerning each other, that we were on the same page, if you take my meaning, then, without the faintest shadow of a doubt, that would be awesome. And I don't mean *like* awesome.

Which brings me to this: Why should I be impressed by the fact that you really really love me? Really? Frankly, I'd prefer that you loved me a little less really, and with more restraint, choosing your words with more deliberation, the way a good poet does. That way, I'll know where I stand.

Same goes for the matter of originality, which is a false requirement in art or love. I do not seek originality in your love any more than in a novel. Why would I choose some wild and crazy fantasy when I could read Alice McDermott? Think of me as your reader. I am happy to do much of the work if you just lay out the stones in the creek, and allow me to leap from one to the other. Music lives between the notes. Writing, between the words. And love in the space you leave me.

If I sing you a song, will you listen? Listen, the way Gretta listens in "The Dead." Songs come and go in the story, many of them, but it is not until Bartell D'Arcy the tenor sings at the end of the evening that we understand what song means to Joyce, and to life. D'Arcy sings "The Lass of Aughrin," about the death of a child—"O, the rain falls on my heavy locks / And the dew wets my skin / My babe lies cold." When he sings, Gretta stops in her tracks on the staircase. She dreams into the past, of growing up near Galway in the west of Ireland, and of the boy, Michael Furey, who at age seventeen died for loving her.

Gabriel watches his wife listen to the singing. So removed is she from the scene of "The Dead"—from the small talk at the dinner party, the gossip, the politics, and the trivial wonders of a self-contained people—that Gabriel does not recognize her, lost in the shadows. Later that night, back at their Dublin Hotel, he asks her about the great sadness in her face. And she tells him of this boy she loved, Michael Furey, whose love for her was so furious and fathomless, that he made the long walk to her house one night in the cold rain, when he was gravely ill, because he wanted to see Gretta again. And he died. "He died for me," Gretta tells her husband.

When she is at last asleep, Gabriel watches her. He realizes he has not loved anyone the way Michael Furey loved, that he has never loved at all. And the story ends with his thinking about the snow that covers Ireland that for his lie. If no one means what is said in love, how are the wolves to be avoided? One can always resort to singing a line or two from Mitchell Parish or Johnny Mercer, I suppose. But at the end of the day, when the underground fingers start scratching from beneath the dungeon floor, truth eventually is known to all the parties concerned. Between language and silence, they traipse about humming songs from the 1960s. "Louie Louie."

I knew a couple who dressed alike, insofar as men and women can dress alike. Same slacks. Same tops. One time, they both wore Dodgers uniforms and looked like baggy clowns. I knew a couple who went on Caribbean cruises. I knew one who practiced witchcraft, and another who practiced hypnosis, and another who practiced the viola. I knew a couple named Tyler and Ali who had nothing in common at all. Same difference.

In eighteenth-century Tunisia, couples were not permitted to speak a word to each other during their first year of marriage. The theory was that after a year passed, when the couple finally spoke, they would have been so conscious of the truth in every situation, that they would speak only the truth from then on. There are no formal records of the failures and successes of Tunisian marriages in the eighteenth century, thus no hard evidence of whether or not the theory was sound.

Only one pertinent document is extant (of course, I'm making this all up), but it is telling in regard to the silent-year law just mentioned. In a diary kept by a young Tunisian woman, she wrote about the day after she and her husband had been married one year. When he finally spoke to her, he kissed her forehead, took her hand, and said, "You're not alone."

I OFFER YOU EVERY CONSIDERATION of gray waves breaking on stones, and a sanctuary of seabirds, glowing like a silk skirt, which I offer you as well, to be employed at grand balls in the springtime, or as a tourniquet for such wounds as you may suffer in battle. I offer several sprigs of berries, red and yellow, a bowl of milk, three George Gershwin and Cole Porter songs, a Mark Helprin novel, stalactites of sun rays, tribal names, an illustrated history of horses, the wreck of an old man's hair, blessings spread out at appropriate intervals, chocolates. You I also offer a battered desk, a stack of unfinished poems written in the high style, to be worked on in the early hours of a winter's day, prints of the American frontier, a deliberately slow Linda Ronstadt version of "Am I Blue?", the aplomb of terns, the virginal light of an early summer evening, a paper plane gliding inches from the floor, then soaring in a loop-de-loop, letters tied in a ribbon, the stillness of a hedge, the stillness of a cord of wood, the stillness of my breath.

From you, in return, I should like a lighthouse beam crossing the path of the moon on a creek, a metropolis of ants in the hollow of an oak tree, a drugstore of the 1940s, a black-and-white soda to go with it, three more Gershwin and Porter tunes, the touch of your naked shoulder, a hunting lodge in the depth of the Northern California forests, a circus of winds on a stormy August afternoon, the slow ascent of the Atlantic. I should also like a patch of ice, a patch of snow, a patch of clarity, my white shirts flapping swanlike on a clothesline, a scythe of light on the roof of a shed, a stone wall in New Hampshire, sudden hills on a long drive in the country, confrontations of hummingbirds, collaborations of green leaves, constellations of ducks, your naked thigh, your patience as I tell my jokes about County Kerry and about the rabbi who walks into a bar, oars at rest in their locks, the tremor of your heart beneath my own.

Stature of ideas is precision of ideas, so let me be precise. You are the earth, to be precise.

A RABBI WALKS INTO A BAR with a parrot on his shoulder. Bartender says, "Where'd you get that?" Parrot says, "Brooklyn. They've got thousands of them."

FIRST KERRY MAN IS WALKING with a sack on his back. Second Kerry man asks, "What have you got in the sack?" First says, "I won't tell ya." Second says, "Ach, do." "All right," says the first. "It's ducks." Second Kerry man says, "If I can guess how many ducks you have in that sack, will you give me one?" First Kerry man says, "I'll give you *both*." Second says, "Five."

SOMETHING A LITTLE OFF about "Dover Beach." Don't you think? I mean, here is Matthew Arnold in Dover on his honeymoon—on his *honeymoon*—and no sooner does he summon his bride to "come to the window," than the woes of the world cave in on his mind, and he wanders into a long, deepening lament about the age. It was 1851, the year Schoefield left his cabin and moved to Canada, and also the year of the Great Exhibition, a festival of English wealth and material advancement. In a way, the destructive self-confidence of the exhibition was a perfect setup for Arnold's fretful poem. He might have appreciated the minor irony that as grand as the national exhibition was, no one remembers it, whereas "Dover Beach" became the most anthologized poem in the world.

And why? Because it laments so beautifully. And Dover was an important place, a connection between major warring civilizations. Not so today, when the village seems spiritless, except in places where history rears its head—Dover Castle, still garrisoned on the white cliffs where the Normans erected it, and the Roman Pharos, a lighthouse tower built in the second century AD. These days, Dover looks like any halfhearted New England port town, with a shopping center filled with dolled-up teenagers, a computer store, and a KFC. The Lord Warden Hotel, where the newly wed Arnolds probably stayed, retains a good look at the sea. It is a customs house now. On a recent morning in April, a boy-faced customs officer plays rock on a tape deck. "I've got you, baby. You've got me."

From a window here 165 years ago, Arnold beheld his progressive, aggressive century, and began serenely: "The sea is calm to-night, / The tide is full, the moon lies fair / Upon the straits . . . Come to the window, sweet is the night-air!" An honored, successful life lay ahead of him. His new bride was nearby. All was well. But by the end of the stanza he was hearing the "eternal note of sadness" in the sea and the rolling of the pebbles, and by the second stanza, the "ebb and flow / Of human misery" was overwhelming. The final lines of "Dover Beach" are racked with disillusionment about a "world which seems" a land of dreams but has "neither joy, nor love, nor light, / Nor certitude, nor peace, nor help for pain." The only way to survive what Arnold in another poem called "this strange disease of modern life" was for lovers, "ah, love," to "be true to one another." I've got you, baby. You've got me.

But here's the thing about the poem. If Arnold was on his honeymoon, with all the thoughtless pleasure the word implies, what was he doing wondering about the disease of modern life? He was supposed to be enjoying a if we wanted to buy it. The kids would have gone bananas at the thought when they were kids. But they were grown by then. We could have our rural fling, without dragging them along. Our friends said they'd never visit if we did it. They would not make the six-hour drive from the city. And we ourselves knew better, having lived in Norwich, Vermont, a snowless year, only to head back to New York at the end of it, giddy with thoughts of escape. We had tired of talking with bears.

But Vermont is known as the place you want to be until you get there. So, there we were, driving up to Grafton two hours ahead of a snowstorm. We'd asked the owners for a weekend's trial. Nice people, they'd said sure. The whole place, all 357 acres, with its frozen pond, its stone bridge, its paddock and nineteen empty stalls, and huge main house with a stone fireplace that soared to the moon—ours for three days. Friday night came the snow. I commandeered the owners' Jeep with the superpowerful headlights and blazing spotlights over the windshield that lit up the frosted fields. We drove to dinner in town, where the jukebox was playing "It's Getting Better" (would you believe it?), and picked up a bottle of cabernet before heading back—the sheets of snow hitting the windshield faster than the wipers could swat them away. We were snow-blind in the tundra, the Klondike.

You know what they say about booze and sex. But they weren't with us when we plopped down on the couch in front of the fire, finished off the bottle, and took off each other's clothes, warm and wilder. Nothing was ever as sweet to the touch as your body, nothing as hungry as your mouth on mine. Did we have music? I can't recall. I remember the wind and snow against the windows, and us against each other, under and over each other, loving while making love, in spite of what they say. Some weekend, eh girl?—though we didn't buy the house. You know what they say about Vermont.

WHY DON'T YOU WRITE of friendship as love? Don't you have friends?

I do. But writing about friendship is difficult. The subject doesn't evoke images. And there's no delirium to friendship, as compared, say, with that night in Vermont.

Oh yes. Love is hysteria.

But friendship is a peaceful little thing. We can go years without speaking to our friends, and the love never falters.

You have men and women as friends?

Mostly men, but several women, too. It's odd, but that sense of peacefulness is exactly the same for both. Take sex out of the picture, and men and women make terrific friends.

Some say that's impossible, to take sex out of the picture.

Not when you're older. In other ways, though, friendship keeps you young, kind of childish. I'm in a club called the Meatheads, a dozen guys who go to bad movies filled with gratuitous violence and no other virtues. We sit in a close-up row, and fling popcorn and Junior Mints at each other across the seats. We're all over sixty.

Friendship isn't always peaceful. Friends fight.

True. But the fights usually settle back to its basic comforting, comfortable state. One time, Coleridge went to visit Wordsworth in his cottage. He walked in, sat down, and did not utter a word for hours. Neither did Wordsworth. When the hours were up, he rose from his chair, and exiting the door, thanked Wordsworth for a perfect evening.

Is friendship isolating?

In a way. I suppose it allows people to be alone with one another. And whether one talks or not, the affection is obvious. Maybe part of the silence comes from an appreciation of the obvious.

Is that why artists rarely touch the subject?

I think so. There's not much to say about it. Once in a while, you'll get a good comrade relationship (Hamlet and Horatio), or a bad one (Brutus and Caesar), but most of the time, the beauty of friendship is undramatic. Gentleness, loyalty, and magnanimity. Sublimely boring. It's why dogs make best friends.

Why does it not evoke images, do you think?

I don't know. Things that evoke images require representation greater than themselves, whereas a friend is a friend. The noun suffices. A creek on most days.

What's that?

It's the only image that comes to mind. Steady and there. A creek on most days.

You call that love?

It is love.

OH, AND IF YOU WERE ABOUT TO ASK why I don't write of love of country, let me beat you to the punch and say, sure I love my country. But nations feed on abstractions. And writers have a hard time with abstractions. America is Mount Rushmore, bulging with freedom, optimism, guilt, redemption, moxie, regeneration, destiny. Destiny? I should embrace destiny? So much easier to hug Americans one by one. Of thee I sing, Trixie, Jose, Jimboy, Alice, Rachel, Sam, and Shauneequa. So much easier to give a squeeze to the stuff that defines us. Baseball, movies, ice cream, songs. Songs. Yes. Forget ice cream. We are the Empire of the Love Song. It's how we rule, our weapon of mass seduction. Under those monumental Mount Rushmore noses, way down below, a boy walks with his dog beside a river, whistling "The Book of Love." Sentimental me. Guess I'll always be.

A TWELVE-YEAR-OLD BOY WALKS with his black lab beside a river in northern Wisconsin. The day is windy and the water rough. The dog sees a duck land on a floating branch and races into the river after it. At once, he is swept downstream. The boy rushes in to save the dog, and he, too, is swept into the river, never to be seen again. The dog meanwhile has clambered up an embankment a hundred yards away. He stands there on alert, looking around for the boy, and barks at the river. After the boy's family has gone into seclusion, after the ministers have finished preaching, after the school is done with counseling and healing, and the TV camera crews have packed up their gear and gone home; after a memorial of flowers and stuffed animals erected at the riverbank has wilted and decayed; after all that, the dog still returns to the place where the boy jumped in to save him. And for years, that is the sound of that place—a prolonged howl curling into the mist that clings to the river.

THE DOG. BY ROGER ROSENBLATT. The dog barks. By Roger Rosenblatt. The dog barks by Roger Rosenblatt, who is trying to read *Crime and Punishment* by Fyodor Dostoyevsky. He is trying to read *Crime and Punishment* by Fyodor Dostoyevsky, but the dog barks. As Raskolnikov dodges his landlady, the dog barks. As Raskolnikov curses his sister's fate, the dog barks, too. The dog always barks. By Rodya Raskolnikov. *Dogs and Punishment* by Rodya Rosenblatt, by Roger Raskolnikov, by Fyodog Dog-stoyevsky. Barkbarkbarkbarkbark.

I am not crazy yet. The dog has not barked me to craziness quite yet. All I have sought to do for the past two days, sitting in the same chair in the same house with the same Hershey's Kisses left over from Halloween at my same left hand—all I have sought is to make some progress with *Crime and Punishment,* and so I have considered killing the dog, as Raskolnikov killed the two old women.

If you kill one dog, after all, what matters it to the balance of the world, if you know what I mean, and I think you do.

What gets me is how little she cares for my peace of mind. I thought she loved me. Does she love me? She has not read *Crime and Punishment.* She knows nothing of the pleasures of listening to Brubeck, while sitting back with Hershey's Kisses on a dismal November afternoon—the trees shorn, the wind mixing with rain—and reading of starving young Russians tormenting themselves in the city of ___, in the year ___. Six long years I have owned this dog, feeding and bathing and tummy-scratching, in return for puppy barking and dog barking. Now she is not six, I remind her. She is forty-two. Time to settle down, I remind her. *Tempus fugit. Cave canem.* Barkbarkbark. She is not the dog I had hoped for, not that dog at all.

Not that I was hoping for Lassie, if that's what you're

thinking. Or Rin Tin Tin, or Yukon King, or Fala, or Checkers, or Him, or Her, nor a dog that flies or takes fingerprints or says "Ruth" in bars. I was not expecting maybe Ms. Magic Dog of the Twenty-first Century, who would not only fetch my copy of *Crime and Punishment,* but who also would have translated the book from the original. Not my dog. Not the dog of my dreams.

All I ever wanted was a good and quiet dog, like the dignified hound in Piero di Cosimo's *Death of Procris,* sitting so mournfully, so nobly at the feet of his fallen mistress. A dog like that would not bark more than once a month (once in his seven). A dog like that would know his place in the order of things, would state by the mere fact of his docile existence that there are those who rule and those who sit quietly, those who read *Crime and Punishment* and those who don't, and therefore do not make it impossible for those who do, just because they hear things that those who do, don't.

Barkbarkbarkbarkbark.

There is nothing out there. I have been stalled on page seventy-one for an hour, and there is nothing out there, while Raskolnikov has axed the two old women over and over again. He feels no remorse. He is consumed with purpose. He can do whatever he wants—sans guilt, sans cairns—he for whom no dog barks.

Would that I were Orpheus, who could speak to animals in their own language. First I would reason with her.

When that didn't work (and it wouldn't), I would threaten her. She would understand me. At my trial, there would be no question that she knew what would befall her if she kept up the racket. Even if the jurors were other dogs, I'd get off. Even if one or two were raccoons, or bears. Polar bear, polar bear, what do you hear?

Now she is still for a moment. The brown, blank eyes fixed with alarm. The head loaded, ready to fire. For the love of God, what can she hear? Is it the sound of an enemy I cannot hear yet? Or is it the sound of the enemy I can never hear, the sound of evil itself, of my own murderous impulse to kill the very dog who barks to keep me from killing the very dog who barks to keep me from killing me?

For the love of God, for the love of Mike. Between the two, I'll take Mike. I can count on Mike. And before you tell me God is love, let me tell you, Mike, too, is love. So are a dozen other friends whom I can think of, off the top of my head. I can count on the love of my friends. But the love of God?

What gets me about God's love is that it's here and gone, once in a while, too flighty for my taste. As the song says, I want a Sunday kind of love. Lasts all through the week. I get why it is that God's kind of love is preferable for theorists; it thrives on low expectations, which some call mystery. I don't want a god of mystery. I want a god I can understand, in terms of justice. "But God loves you categorically. God loves everybody." Whoo-hoo. But does he really care what happens to you? Or to the victims of the Great Fire of London, and the Triangle Shirtwaist Factory fire? Or to bring things up-to-date, the dead children in Syria and Sandy Hook? "He cares. He just doesn't interfere." Seriously? Call that a god? If we're talking gods, give me the Greek and Roman gang. They may have been slobs. But those gods could *do* something.

May I ask you, Mr. God, what happened to you since the Greeks and the Romans? If you don't mind my saying so, or even if you do, you used to have balls. People behaved poorly? You drowned them. Pharaoh acted up? You tormented him, and Job, too, who didn't deserve any of it. You let him have it to make a point. When was it exactly that you became a divine pussy, James Joyce's pretty boy, sitting back and paring your fingernails? I'd like you to lift a finger. You did it for Michelangelo. Why not for us?

On TV tonight, I watched a clip of a biplane in an air show, with a daredevil woman standing on its top wing. Over a loudspeaker came the announcement that the woman was going to attempt the feat of retaining her standing position as the plane did a 360. The clip showed the woman steadying herself as the plane began its roll. Just then, a wind blew out of nowhere, the pilot lost control, and he and the woman hit the ground in flames, consuming the biplane directly in front of an audience that included children, perhaps the woman's own two children. God, were you there?

Would that you and the imagination were one, as Wallace Stevens said, so that we might imagine what we know, and believe in the goodness we imagine.

Would that you did not conceal yourself, but rather showed your face to the rationalists and the faithful alike, bringing both to order.

Would that you shed a light so much greater than the sun, there were no shadows anywhere.

AND YET: Light is the shadow of God (Plato). And still: The greatest of these is love (Corinthians).

MARTHA, JESUS, AND LAZARUS went for a walk. There was a trinity for you. One the beseecher, one the divine magician, and one the poor stunned sap who, no sooner had he heard the earth shoveled on his coffin lid, then shazzam, he was on his feet again, asking, "'Sup with that?" Lots of questions about their story. Why Martha? Why Lazarus? And why did Jesus weep? Love was sweeping the country that day, no doubt about it, for the only reason for Jesus's tears was his love, not for Lazarus—he hardly knew the guy, for Chrissake—but rather for all the Lazaruses and their families and everyone, high and low.

They call that tale a miracle, and it was, though not because Jesus hauled a dead man back to life. The miracle was that he loved him enough to do it.

BUT WERE YOU *THERE*? In the final days of the Warsaw Ghetto, the imprisoned Jews knew the game was up. They had seen their families and friends carted off to the extermination camps or dying of hunger or diphtheria, and they understood that fate was theirs. Still, they got hold of pieces of paper, on which they wrote messages, poems, anecdotes, thoughts, sentiments, and fragments of autobiography. Then they rolled the pieces of paper into tiny scrolls and slipped them in the crevices of the ghetto walls. Why? Why do it? They had no contact with the outside world. For all they knew, their scrolls, if found at all, would be discovered by their Nazi captors, who would laugh at their efforts, and destroy them. Nothing on earth would be left of the Jews in the Warsaw Ghetto. So why did they bother? Because they had to. They had a story to tell, and they had to tell a story.

Some years ago, Jean-Dominique Bauby, the editor of the French magazine *Elle,* suffered a stroke so massive, it paralyzed his entire body except for his left eyelid. Yet with that one movable eyelid, he signaled the alphabet, with which he spelled out individual words, then sentences, and eventually a memoir, *The Diving Bell and the Butterfly.*

In the book *The Perfect Storm,* we see a fisherman on a mackerel schooner going down in a hurricane. There is no doubt he's a goner. Still, by lantern light, he writes out a message that he places in a bottle, and flings it out to sea. Just as the Russian submariners in the 1990s wrote letters to their wives, children, friends, and sweethearts, and placed them in capsules that rose to the surface, though they could not.

My goodness! What story could be so urgent that we must tell it in the face of death, as our last gestures in the universe, with our blinking eyes and sea-soaked hands? Why, a love story, of course.

My heart is my theology, which makes me a glad parishioner, wide-eyed as a boy with a cowlick, a sucker, if you must know. I would be the first to volunteer to whitewash Tom Sawyer's fence. I'd enjoy doing it, too, happily aware that I'd be hornswoggled, because to my way of thinking, there would be no swoggling of the horn. Even if I caught a little smirk from Tom, I would not give a hoot. I'd take to every crooked slat in that fence, and to the frayed posts as well, as if the whole thing were a canvas begging to be turned into a masterpiece. Let me at it, I'd tell Tom, because, you know, you're right: Whitewashing this old fence is the most enviable enterprise in the world. Without such an attitude, how would one ever fall in love? What other way is there for one to fall in love? And the morning would wear on, and soon the fence would glow like a silk skirt. I would revise the fence. I'd hum. And Tom would watch me, pity mixed with mirth, and murmur, There's one born every minute. And I would think, I hope so.

Mr. Duncan, the lover of things, stopped by Tiffany's one afternoon to pick up a wife. He bought a good one, very pretty, very nice. While he was in the store, he bought three kids as well, two girls and a boy. All three were clean, bright and well behaved. He bought them "to go," and returned with his goods to a penthouse apartment he had just purchased in Trump Tower, which he had recently furnished with antiques, eighteenth-century English for the most part, and with three Picassos, two Magrittes, and five Old Masters, one Velázquez and four Vermeers. He had bought them from the Met, the Louvre, and the Prado, which he also bought while visiting Spain. Then he bought Spain. Visitors to his home remarked favorably upon his art collection, and on his wife and children. They also liked the singing and piano playing of Michael Feinstein, whom Mr. Duncan acquired, as he often said, for a song, and from whom he repeatedly requested two tunes: "I Got Plenty of Nothin'" and "Mine." Everyone seemed disposed toward Mr. Duncan. Strangers tipped their hats to him. Philanthropies and political campaign officials called upon him frequently. The president invited him for a round of golf. Donald Trump himself paid a visit to his penthouse, which Mr. Trump called the greatest penthouse in the world. Together they sang "All You Need Is Love"—da da da da da.

Late one summer evening, Mr. Duncan stood on the terrace of his penthouse, and looked down upon the city and its people, so many of whom had heard of Mr. Duncan and who associated his name with wealth and happiness. Chock full o'Nuts had included him in its jingle—"Better coffee Mr. Duncan's money can't buy." Mr. Duncan was not amused, and bought better coffee to prove his point. Then he looked back into the apartment and the many possessions he had acquired, including his wife and children, and a black lab named Duncan who came whenever his master called, and who begged and also heeled. There was a mistress as well, whom he had purchased last week in Bloomingdale's and whom he would phone after his family was asleep. For now he was content to survey his property, and speculate about how many more things he could acquire before he died. Who said money can't buy you love? he asked no one in particular. And no one in particular answered him.

YOU WOULDN'T KNOW IT, but I've been clearing out the weeds. Came upon the first inkling of a rose last Saturday, and a bee breathing in the arriving season. Soon the rest of the flowers will ignite. Why I think of kettles blowing steam beats me. Maybe it's those songs they were playing on the car radio the other day. "It Might as Well Be Spring." And "Younger Than Springtime." The road to the beach is losing its grip. Soon it will turn to sand, and slide into the ocean, the way the young woman slid from a climbing rope and fell to her death into a snowy ravine, in that Sylvester Stallone movie we walked out on. Eventually everything loses its grip. I may be losing mine.

I have been invited to give a reading at a college in Kentucky. I'm thinking of telling them a story I've started writing about a woman in the 1850s in northern Vermont, who opened her front door and found her drunken husband, and who, when he stormed in demanding their little boy, and threatening them both, and clapping her on the side of the head, took a shotgun and blew his chest away, so that his head fell to his legs. She wound up in Kentucky. That's the tie-in. What do you think? Too rough? I need you in moments like this, my most exacting editor. I need you in most moments. Did you say I've got a lot to learn?

From my crazy father's head I sprang—you know that—for good and ill. I inherited the rants. You remember. Still, on the whole, madness has gone better than I anticipated. Crazy as I get, I'm a cucumber salad compared with the army generals on TV who speak of collateral damage, as if death were a cucumber salad. Years ago, I proposed a story to my editor at *Time*—I've probably told you about this—in which I would go around the world and try to quantify war. What I wanted to do was to weigh everything that went into the preparation for wars everywhere. Every contributing item—cannon, fighter jets, tanks, cluster bombs, oak-leaf clusters, rockets, the VA hospitals, the cartridges, uniforms, the epaulets, the spit and polish, the splints and crutches. The idea was to add up all this stuff, determine the tonnage, and then speculate about a world unburdened.

My editor, a good guy, considered my proposal, and eventually said no. But I always liked wondering how light the world would feel, with all that killing material off its shoulders. Nothing left but love songs about spring, and inept men puttering around gardens, missing their wives. And since there would be no wars, there would be no need for war photographers either, and the shutterbugs could turn their attention to the weeds, the roses, and the bees.

Life is a picnic, you said. I said, the hell it is. But you insisted. Life is a picnic, with sandwiches and chips, on a grassy hill, under a tree, with Coke and beer, and chocolate chip cookies, and oatmeal raisin, too. Music is carried up from the village—the theme song from *Picnic,* now that you mention it—and everyone is chatting and laughing, everyone being the two of us. You know? says the girl. I think life is a picnic. You know? says the boy. I think you're right.

Not enough is made of happiness, you said. I said, Are you serious? But, to make your point, you indicated the geese fluttering in the road, and the sea, which you described as rearing up like horses. You breathed in the brine, which invaded your hair. You sang "Younger Than Springtime," and urged me to sing along with you, until I gave in, and we belted the song as if we were a pair of Technicolor sweethearts in a Rodgers and Hammerstein show. They gave us a room in Barbados that had an unimpeded view of the hotel Dumpster. It doesn't get any better than this, you said.

Down by the glen I met a maid
Eyes brown as upturned soil had she
I said, like that, will you marry me?
And on my arm her head she laid.

A Vermont woman goes to the door and sees her husband, drunk and red-faced and shaking his fists. The year is 1851, the year of "Dover Beach" and the Great Exhibition. She attempts to shut the door on her husband, but he plants his boot on the threshold and thrusts himself inside.

William! He shouts for his son. William! The boy cowers and remains hidden in a storeroom in the cellar. When the woman tries to place her body in front of her husband, he slaps her on the side of the head with an open hand, claps her like a bell, and knocks her to the floor. There is blood on her teeth. Her husband starts for the cellar stairs. William! The woman hauls herself up and goes to the hall umbrella stand, where she keeps a shotgun. Her husband turns to face her. He has time to see her load the shotgun, but no time to do anything about it. She aims at his chest and shoots him twice, both barrels. His chest is blown away, so that his head drops to his legs before all parts of him fall to the floor. The woman rushes to get her son, and together the two of them run from the house, never to look back. After many travels, they establish a home in McGowan, Kentucky, a small town where the cream-filled doughnut was invented, and where, many years later, Elvis introduced "Sweet Caroline." The woman changes her name and finds work as a seamstress. Her boy attends the local school, and for the rest of their lives, all is safe and well. She never remarries. At the end of her life, William asks her, Did you love my father? *Love* him? she says. I loved him to *death*.

ADMIT IT, YOU WANTED TO shoot me that afternoon I came home with that girl's perfume on my shirt. I forget her name, if I ever knew it. All right, it was Sheila. But kiss me is all she did. All right, I kissed back. Yet kiss me is all you did. So I accounted for my morning, and explained to you that Rhodesian pygmies captured me and took me blindfolded to their cave in the Black Forest, where they made fun of my haircut and played board games without rules. One of them had no eyebrows. Another had hair like turf. (I could make them out through the blindfold.) Their leader was a picaroon married to a flirtatious milliner, whom everyone flattered but no one took seriously. It was she who slathered me with her perfume. I remembered little else, save that there were bleating sheep in the middle distance, and a great many inconsequential business dealings going on, which were adjudged urgent, nonetheless. After enduring many torments, such as a string of unfunny knock-knock jokes told me by the milliner, I managed to loosen my ties and cast off the blindfold. Then I returned home to you who kissed me.

My father kissed me on my wedding day. He reached up, took my head in both hands, and kissed me in the middle of my forehead. He must have kissed me when I was a baby, but the wedding-day kiss is the only one I recall. That is how it went with him. He showed no affection for his parents, who showed no affection for him. He showed none for his younger brother, an estate lawyer. He showed open contempt for extended members of our family, of whom there were few, and whom we saw rarely. He showed a sort of stewardship affection for my younger brother, and the affection of companionability for my mother. His affection for me seemed intertwined with one or another of my so-called achievements, as well as with how they might be presented to others. That came after my high school years, during which I had refused to open a book, and divided my valuable time between girls and sports. He was both contemptuous and flabbergasted at the waste I was making of my life. Later, after I reformed, he liked me a bit more. In his office, he framed an op-ed piece I wrote for the *New York Times,* so that his patients either could be impressed by the piece, or by the fact that a son of his produced it. I was never sure if he loved me or some of the things I did. I don't know how much I loved him, either.

His only friends were patients and doctor cronies, whom I thought he liked, until something arose that allowed him to reveal he never liked them at all. An elder doctor used to invite him to go deep-sea fishing at his home in Smithtown, Long Island. He took me with him, and I was pleased to observe the camaraderie of the men, as we putted out into the bay for sea bass and blues. I thought my father regarded his elder colleague affectionately as a mentor. One day he told me of a farmer whom the colleague had referred to him, saying something to the effect that he was recommending my father even though he was Jewish. I was stunned. But my father told the tale as if to say, this is what one is to expect of life.

I was sort of stunned by my dad himself, the way one is stunned by Stonehenge or the Grand Tetons. He was so orderly and self-contained that most of his affections seemed directed toward habit and custom. He had one way of looking, formal. He had one way of greeting people, distanced, and one way he expected to be greeted, respectful. He had certain things he liked, all traditional, and many more things he disliked, such as informality, sloppy dress, improper familiarity, such as the uninvited use of first names, and willful chaos. Thus he disliked liberals. We argued about these matters, and up to the point of an explosive rage, he seemed to enjoy debate. I fought as well as I could, but I don't think he loved me more or less for the effort. Ginny he seemed to love more than anyone.

Even our first two children, Carl and Amy—John was born after Dad died of a heart attack at the age of sixty-eight—were given a cautionary and conditional love. The love of one who delights in observing puppies. I think he would have loved the children more fully and expressively if he could have, but he lacked practice. Amy tickled him because of her rebel's streak. Yet he gave her the nickname Bella Abzug, who in both style and manner represented all he loathed in American politics. Amy was too young to understand or care.

From time to time, in my college years, I observed his silences at home. He would sit in his dark green wing chair reading history books, usually about the Civil War, or in front of the TV, watching lawyer shows. Medical shows he could not abide. His large, not quite bald head barely moved. He said nothing, as though he was unaware that he was not alone. At our wedding reception he was gregarious with the guests with the aggressive bonhomie of a maître d'. I had seen him put on that face a few times before, and I cringed at the act. An hour or so earlier, as the wedding party was assembling for the procession, he drew me aside, reached up, took my head in both hands, and kissed me.

You two go on doing whatever it is parents are supposed to be doing, and I'll just look out the window, pretending you are interested in me. Oh, see. A parade, at the center of which Abe Lincoln rides a float festooned with red, white, and blue bunting, and surrounded by cartwheeling boys and girls. Such a privilege to get a glimpse of Honest Abe at my age, nine, and to appreciate that I, too, can grow up to be president or Babe Ruth. Abe or the Babe. Beyond Mr. Lincoln lie the smokestacks of the Spaldeen factory, burning pink rubber, and spewing balls out into the street. They spook the horses. Beyond the factory sway trees at appropriate intervals, breathing laboriously in the wind, and beyond them, other children in various scenes of play. In the far distance, maybe a hundred miles away, I see a window much like mine, and within it a boy my age seated at a baby grand. From the fingering I can tell he's playing "Where Is Love?" When he finishes, he goes to the window, and peers in my direction. But by now the fog has rolled in off the Atlantic, and no one can see anything.

This might be as good a time as any to decide whether or not you love me. But there's no rush.

He breaks one's heart, Don Draper, the lead character played by Jon Hamm in the TV series *Mad Men,* principally because his own heart was broken in childhood, because his prostitute mother who died when he was born did not want him, and his harsh father died shortly afterward. He has spent his adult life trying to eradicate his childhood, to the point of adopting the identity of a dead comrade-in-arms in Korea, the real Don Draper. Our man is lost. He does bad things, he does good things. But, in spite of appearances, and the handsome looks of a comic book superhero before he changes into costume, he has no control over his life. This is the way of the unloved child. You can make up for practically any other deficiency, but that particular omission runs through you like a spear. Wherever you go after that, however smart you are or successful you seem, you're still a goner.

Don Draper, Bill Clinton, and JFK went for a walk. Where is love, the three men sang. I always had the feeling that Bill Clinton was driven by that question, and quest, to the extent that no evident love given him, by Hillary or Chelsea, or by his many friends, or by the extracurricular women, or by the entire world, was sufficient to make up for an unloved beginning. Same goes for JFK, who seemed to be reared in a boarding school rather than a family, with a manic father, and all the Kennedy kids sleeping in different beds in Hyannisport from night to night, never one of their own. People said that the extramarital lurchings of both men were propelled by an overwrought appetite for sex. I doubt it. What's sex got to do with it? I think they were looking for love, as another song goes, just like Don Draper, and as was said in "My Last Duchess," their looks went everywhere. They could never get enough, because early on, they got too little.

Lost and deeper lost, Don Draper travels around like Ulysses in a suit, and like Ulysses, he sleeps with every woman within reach. Only one woman stays out of reach, sexually—Anna, the widow of the real Don Draper, with whom he makes a pact that allows him to keep Draper's name and history. She, in turn, becomes a sort of mother to Don. She encourages him, consoles him, and gives unjudging love. He buys her a house, as a good son would. He visits her in California, whenever he's in trouble, like the prodigal. She lights up at the sight of him. When he

this year—oddly, because I had been thinking about my mother less and less as her condition deteriorated, and as she grew less and less herself. A mighty impressive disease, Alzheimer's. It takes your breath away, first as it inflicts progressive shocks on the victim's system, and then, on the victim's relatives and loved ones, as it deadens feeling altogether.

The disease so completely becomes the sufferer, one isn't sure if one is supposed to attend the patient or the illness. Such fascinating stages. Initially there is a kind of troubled yet sweet awareness that the clock of the patient's mind is a few seconds off. Then an encroaching recognition of loss of function becomes less recognition and greater loss. Soon words and phrases are looped, like mad lines from a postmodern play; then Tourette's-like bursts, frags, some incomprehensible, some vile; then less of that, less of everything, until the mind is concentrated down to a fretful stare. Even in death, my mother's face looked worried.

At this time of year, I ought not to think about her. I should be thinking of China and Syria. I should be thinking about the Taliban. There's *Mad Men* and *Breaking Bad* to think about, and the start of the baseball season; Jeter's injury, Pettitte's comeback. I should be thinking of spring and April: T. S. Eliot, Shakespeare, taxes, Oklahoma City, Jesus, Moses, Al Jolson singing "April Showers." My mother used to sing that. Her birthday fell on April 1. No fooling.

But I am not really thinking about her, either. I am thinking about not thinking about her, and feeling neither guilt nor responsibility. Now, here's a feat for Alzheimer's: It takes guilt away from a Jew! If I converted to Catholicism, would I get some back? Sometimes I feel I'd like to convert to Catholicism, which makes repentance easier, but why bother *them*?

I do not feel accountable. I did my filial duties, lovingly, for the most part. Alzheimer's drops in from nowhere, like a mistimed curtain. You don't catch it because you went outside in winter without a hat. The trouble is, I don't feel anything, save the shadows of memories, and even they have to be reconstructed willfully.

The thing about Alzheimer's is that if it lasts long enough, it takes away everything, not only by erasing the person you once knew but also by erasing the you you knew, too, leaving two carcasses. When the disease began to worsen, I used to tell myself that while I could make neither head nor tail of my mother's ravings, still she might have been clear as daylight to herself. When she caved in to silence, I told myself she might be harboring pleasant, unexpressed thoughts. Eventually I stopped kidding myself. What I saw of her was what I got: a blank stone in a wall eaten away by rain.

Which is very much the way I feel now. The people around Alzheimer's victims suffer from secondhand smoke, and the worst of their secondary disease is that, after the long years, the one thought, the one plea that overtakes all others—before all the resurrected laughter, the walks along the beach in Chatham on Cape Cod, the brassy imitation of Mae West's strut, the home-sewn Dracula costume at Halloween, the bewildered attendance at my basketball games, the singing of "April Showers"—is: die.

And so, she did. And spring is sprung. And because hope breathes eternal, even if nothing else does, I am wondering if my mother is somewhere up and about, breathing again, where life is restored and the air and mind are clear.

HERE'S WHAT I THINK about Cyrano. Not that you asked. What I think, in a nutshell, is that his unattractiveness, the fear and contempt in which he was held by men and women alike, had nothing to do with his nose. To the contrary, I think folks found his nose alluring, prominent, and elegant, a doozy of a nose, and that women especially found it sexy, irresistible in its way, an educated and sophisticated nose, a nose for all seasons. Cyrano, appearing to hold a different opinion, out-dueled the nitwits who mocked him, and hid from the women he yearned for. But I think this was all bullshit. It wasn't the nose that scared the girls away; it was the force of his passion. What's more, I think he recognized this, and so lent his passion to others for delivery. Size matters. A lot of girls can't take a heart that big.

HERE'S WHAT I THINK about Heathcliff. I am Heathcliff. No, I'm not. And who would want to be. To be sure, the novel makes one hell of a love story, you have to give it that. Catherine cries, I am Heathcliff, projecting the ultimate statement of oneness in love—the passionate, insatiable longing to be made whole by the existence of the other person. The becoming of the other person. A bit heavy, for my taste. I know that these two are soul-deep in love with each other. But do they love each other? Do they even like each other? I doubt it. It's all too hot to handle. Too close, too close for comfort.

And what sort of statement of purpose do they give the world? Tea for two, and us for us. They make their own rules. And it gets more than a little creepy, as Heathcliff seeks to "absorb" Catherine's corpse into his body, determined that they "dissolve" into each other. Forget about anyone else. Forget death. All that matters is personal desire. They're each other's addicts. My romance doesn't need a thing but you.

Makes you wonder what would happen if Heathcliff and Catherine went to one of those oh-so-sophisticated cocktail parties one reads about, where the couples toss their house keys in the center of the room, and the husbands go off with other men's wives, and vice versa. Pity the guest who winds up with one of Brontë's breathless duo.

"Who did you get last night?"

"That Heathcliff. Never again!"

C. Day Lewis called their passion "the essential isolation of the soul, or rather two halves of a single soul, forever sundered and struggling to unite." I've got you under my skin.

Here's what I think about the Chinese and their clock. You don't forget something important to you unless it isn't important. So there.

One by one they were all becoming shades. Better pass boldly into that other world, in the full glory of some passion, than fade and wither dismally with age.

—JAMES JOYCE, "THE DEAD"

The airports are closed due to a heightened awareness of lovers worldwide, who are consuming everyone's attention as if it were consommé. What shall we do about this—what should one call it—threat? Terrorists will be terrorists, the little devils. The Taliban will be Talibananas. Lovers will be lovers, that's a given. The world will always welcome them, etc. etc., but there is such a thing as overabundance, you know. You can't have too many terrorists, but lovers reproduce like rabbits, and if you're not watching them every second, they will take the attention of the world away from the bombers and the bludgeoners, if you can imagine such a thing. So, I ask you, comrade, what is to be done?

Am I making sense? I apologize. It won't happen again. Another lapse of judgment. Or was it taste? In any event, a lapse. I did not mean to make sense. I meant to get you on a slow boat to China. No need to pack. We'll just wear bathing suits and toothbrushes. I'll learn Chinese, and you'll do jigsaw puzzles on the poop deck. Or we could stay home and order out. Chinese?

See here, lilacs. Let's dig in and bring a new aroma to the places where creeks go slack, and the animals sleep their deep deep sleep. Let us overrun these places. Every lover knows them. I'm talking Don Juan. I'm talking Don Draper. I'm talking Lancelot and Casanova and Casanosa and Cyranose. After all, in the long run, when it comes down to it, in the final analysis, no one is gulled by death-talk. Lovers rule. And he who knows the geography of hearts, if given the opportunity, will praise the overrun. Let's live unhinged.

LET'S FALL IN LOVE. For if I loved you, time and again you would hear me say that I want to be loved by you, by you, and nobody else but you. This I have told every little star, and the blue moon, too, in the blue skies, though I can't remember where or when. Or where is love? Where *is* love? Under moonlight in Vermont, or on the moon over Miami, or in autumn in New York, or April in Paris? What is this thing called love? I love you for sentimental reasons, perhaps because you are the promised breath of springtime and I cherish the very thought of you. Why won't you believe me? It's you I adore—Laura, Marie, Mary, and Mustang Sally. Come rain or come shine, I thought about you. You were always on my mind, in the wee small hours of the morning. Sincerely. So, Maybelline, won't you change partners and dance with me? Otherwise, I'll be all alone by the telephone, dancing in the dark, time after time, as time goes by. They laughed at me wanting you, body and soul. But it's very clear: Our love is here to stay. So let me call you sweetheart? It had to be you, you and the night and the music.

HALLOWEEN. SOON THE CREEK will tarnish with the moon, and chimney smoke will rise in tubes along the coast. Not cold enough for indoor fires yet. The season vacillates, while the more instinctive animals prepare for frost. Where do rabbits go in winter? To tunnel-land, I guess, like the Vietcong. The sea grass tilts eastward. The deer grow bolder, or more desperate, making skittish stampedes across our yellow lawn. The ocean is gray. The air is gray. The graying of America. At a corner table in one of the few restaurants to stay open this late in the year, a couple sits speechless with a cup of coffee between them. Where do restaurants go in winter?

If this weren't home, I'd be out of here, to Florida, or the islands. Like Saint Martin. I could hole up there and play outdoors chess with deserters from the French Foreign Legion, near the pier in Marigot. I could seek a psychic, who will assure me, in French, that I am destined to meet a black-haired native beauty, who is bound to break my heart. She will laugh at the old Legionnaires I play chess with. They will laugh at me behind my back. She will tell me, as she walks out on our two rooms above the shells and postcards shop, that I lack imagination. I am of another order, she will say. Who could argue with her. The Frenchmen will smile coldly. About suffering, the old bastards were never wrong.

Shall we gather the evil spirits together on this night, and drive them off? Halloween. I think of "Clay," Joyce's Halloween story of death and irritation. Out on our deck, I stare leeward, listening to the Atlantic chug like a train. The wind passes over my mind like a witch. It mauls me, then flies on. Motion is the principal element of the universe, after all. Witches can no more stop in their tracks than can sharks in the water around Saint Martin. Remember the shark we saw here last summer? Not thirty feet from shore. Big dark mother. We watched it lumber.

If you must know, I wasn't really thinking about you

until now. And now, you are all I am thinking about. If the local kids come round for candy, I'll choose trick, hoping that they can do magic, like witches, and make you appear. The skiff nudges the dock like a dog's nose. And I head for bed.

WAS IT FOR THIS I uttered prayers
And sobbed and cursed and kicked the stairs,
That now, domestic as a plate,
I should retire at half-past eight?
—EDNA ST. VINCENT MILLAY, "GROWN-UP"

YOU ARE TOO BEAUTIFUL, the young man sings to himself as he mounts the steps of the New York Public Library, and catches sight of her reading beside the lion on the left. Is there anything lovelier than a woman lost in a book, he wonders, at the same time realizing he is hardly the first person to make such an observation. But originality is not his aim. In fact, he feels oddly comfortable knowing that he was thinking something that others had thought before him. He is a writer, as yet unpublished, but a writer still. Here at the library a writer can stand in the company of all who had ever written. And the picture of this young woman—her hair the color of cherrywood, her eyes lowered upon the pages of (he makes a guess) *Piers Plowman*—

both thrills and delights him so completely, he trips and nearly topples from the stone steps on his head.

Did you know—he is about to approach her with a line, he is fairly certain, no one has ever used before. Did you know, miss, that this library used to be the site of the Croton Dispensing Reservoir, which received water from the Croton Reservoir upstate by way of forty miles of pipes, and delivered it, by means of more pipes, to all the homes and businesses of Manhattan? Why no, I did not know that, she will say. My goodness, she will say. A reservoir in the center of the city, she will say. What's more, he will go on, the reservoir covered eight acres, and was surrounded by a stone wall fifty feet high, with a twenty-five-foot-wide walking path at the top. Citizens would take Sunday promenades around the structure. Edgar Allan Poe walked here. He wrote of it. So interesting, she will say, looking at the young man's face with a gentle wonder similar to the one she was bestowing on *Piers Plowman* a moment before.

Would you be disappointed to learn that the young man does not approach the young woman to speak of the reservoir? He has it in mind to add to his factual report the poetic observation that the reservoir that had slaked the thirst of the city then gave way to the library which addressed the city's thirst for knowledge. Would you be disappointed to know that he fails to say that to her? Me, too. For the two of them, when apprehended from a distance, appear to be made for each other. And this certainly seems possible in the imagination of the young man mounting the steps. But that, he tells himself, is where I should like to keep this story—in my imagination. For all I know, he tells himself, there is no woman near the lion, reading. And no library.

Your mission, should you choose to accept it, is to love your enemy.

That's what W. D. Snodgrass said: to love your enemy. But that's impossible.

Mission impossible.

Not for people like Snodgrass, I suppose. Not for gentle souls. But I'm not a gentle soul.

What gets your goat, exactly, that makes such love impossible? Treachery? Dirty tricks?

Yes. Little people doing little things. Duck bites. But there's a slew of the grand malefactors, too. Enemies of the world. Führers. Pol Potheads. Idi-ots. Why should one love them?

What else do you have to give them, that will not destroy you in the bargain?

Hate destroys the hater? I don't know about that. Hate often is simply a show of good judgment.

So is love. Love shows better judgment. Love is freedom.

Not of choice. Snodgrass says, "You cannot choose but love."

He means that as a fact of life, not a restriction.

He was too gentle.

No one is too gentle.

ONE OF THESE DAYS the cops will haul me in for looking at people. I can't help it, officer. It's their faces—their helpless, gutsy, mellow, pleading, earnest faces. En masse. Lovable. Oh, I know. People do not get along well in groups. It's the curse of the species, evolution stopping just short of civilization. And certainly there's nothing lovable about a lynch mob or a mob of customers pursuing a bargain sale at JCPenney, for instance. Those deadly masses one does not stare at with anything but horror and despair.

Yet there are others. That crowd of 6,500 that evening at the Chautauqua amphitheater, rapt at a concert of Brahms—their faces, half in shadow, alert as if they had just received startling good news. That crowd of 14,000 in Moscow, in the 1980s, listening to every word of Voznesensky's poems, eager to catch some subversive nuance. Or that crowd of elders on the lawn in Tanglewood, listening to Previn playing "The Second Time Around."

When I was working at *Time,* I used to watch the crowds on the Avenue of the Americas. Brave squadrons, striding from home to work, slouching from work to home. The pictures on the TV news of refugees in Africa. Sebastião Salgado's photographs of gold miners in Brazil. Ansel Adams's shot of the family in Appalachia. Let us now praise unknown men and women. Even a flash mob on the Brooklyn Bridge. Silly. Sweet.

Throngs at a ball game. Take me out to them. Throngs in the museums, subways, on the beaches. Thousands, millions, in their anonymous assertions. Light vanishes into light. Same flesh. Same bone.

HOW TO LOVE minor hotel employees: In the hotel lobby I spotted a cardboard sign posted on an easel, announcing a meeting that day of a group involved with the economics of veterinary medicine. The event was titled "Practice and Progress." In the upper right-hand corner of the sign was a yellow Post-it that read, PUT THIS UP IMMEDIATELY.

Let us now praise the person to whom that Post-it was directed. Whoever it is waits for orders from the hotel management to put up cardboard signs announcing future meetings. He probably has many duties at this level of significance. Once receiving his orders, he acts on them promptly—PUT THIS UP IMMEDIATELY—lest he lose his job and paycheck to someone who follows orders faster and better. (I am using "he" though "she" is just as likely.) Faster means immediately. Better means that one must be careful to position the poster and the easel in the center of the hotel lobby, where the greatest number of people might see it, especially the members of the organization interested in the economics of veterinary medicine.

Clearly, the person has done the job as instructed. Otherwise, there would be no sign and easel in the center of the lobby. Yet, consciously or unconsciously, the unseen and unacknowledged sign-putter-upper left the Post-it on his handiwork. You and I know why. Because without the Post-it there would be no evidence that the person who put up the sign existed. The Post-it gives notice of a life. And that life is more important than the sign or the easel or the lobby. Even more important than the economics of veterinary medicine, no matter how much progress the practice has made.

HOW TO LOVE the rest of the world. Instructions included in this kit come in French, Spanish, German, and Japanese, as well as in 6,706 other languages, the total number of the world's distinct languages. But don't let that throw you. Don't let anything about the enterprise throw you. You can do it, anyone can do it, because one doesn't learn to love the world in one shot. Rather, start out loving ten or fifteen thousand people at a clip. After a few years, that number will grow to the millions, and include those who have dodged the Census Bureau and the chess-playing

Legionnaire deserters in Saint Martin, as well as the Japanese soldiers from World War II who still are hiding in Saipan, in the trees. In no time, you will be loving the entire world's population, all 7.106 billion of the bastards. What do you think of that?

What you want to do next is to make a study of the species. This kit includes copies of *Don Quixote, Paradise Lost, King Lear,* every Dickens novel, and *The Great Gatsby,* in all the aforementioned languages, which you should read slowly and carefully. Then, turn to that part of *Specimen Days* in which nurse Walt Whitman is tending the Union fallen and near-dead in the U.S. Patent Office in Washington, DC. The Patent Office doubled as a hospital in the Civil War. Whitman notes that the same species capable of coming up with the most dazzling inventions made of wood and brass was just as capable of blowing off one another's limbs. The hall was filled with bright machines lying side by side with men on cots, massaging their new stumps.

The final step, when you have finished your reading, is to take a walk to the creek. There a family of swans has sequestered itself under the drawbridge near the NO WAKE sign, and the light has stalled above the open mouth of the creek, so that the sun burns like a coal in ash, and the summer wind is a rumor on your face. You will find that you weep from wonder and remorse. Then go and treat the wounded.

Accidents will happen, she says, forgiving his hand for brushing against her breast. They had been dancing to a faster beat, but then the band slowed, and they, hardly more than strangers, were as close as can be, as though they were in an embrace, treading water in the North Atlantic after a shipwreck. The ship had just gone down, and there they were, cold and soaked, clinging to each other in the dark. Now he apologizes again, and tries to establish a little distance, not knowing how much distance to maintain after the breast incident, actually not knowing anything about her at all, or about the two of them together, thrown together. Their date had been arranged by an online matchmaking service, name of Bliss. Bliss had taken note of their vitals, and done the math, and Bliss had set them up for an evening of dinner and dancing. Each of them thought, I'm too old for this. She forty-five, he forty-one. Each of them came close to calling off the whole thing, and both would have done so were it not for the prospect of another night of Netflix, and the inevitable phone message: "It's Mom, dear." Now they move warily to "Dancing in the Dark," occasionally catching each other's eyes, mostly looking around the old ballroom with the echo and the spinning lights. She dreams she has forgotten how to use her body. He dreams he has forgotten her name.

HEGEL, THAT OLD TROUBLEMAKER, speculated that if all the dreams experienced within a certain time frame, such as an era or an age, were recorded, they would constitute the true history of that period, more so than straightforward history. Who knows? But the gathering of evidence would be fun. No? Everyone would be required to record his dreams at the moment of awakening, and various chroniclers would be assigned to gather up the pieces every morning and bring them to a distribution center. The dreams station. Dreams Central. There they would place the collected dreams in some sort of order—alphabetical, chronological, longitudinal—or better still, in no order whatever, since, after all, they are dreams. And they would be read aloud every evening by a town crier type to a waiting throng in a public square, or a plaza, a place like that, to listen to a recitation of the truth. The recorded dreams would tell them all they need or want to know about where they stood in the universe.

If jobs in this imagined world were up for grabs, I would like to be one of the public readers of the dreams, to enable me to see the pleasure and puzzlement in the faces of my fellow citizens as I recount, say, the domination of pelicans, lawns turned white by moonlight, the triumph of enemies, appointments missed, and all the other elements of which dreams are typically composed. Would the whole thing get old hat, I wonder. Dreams are supposed to be unique to every dreamer, unlike the samenesses of the wakened world. Would they sound unique when tossed into the company of others' dreams, day after day? Would we grow bored with history as dreams, and yearn for good old-fashioned, tried-and-true history again?

I don't think so. We know there's no such thing as good old-fashioned, tried-and-true history, but we believe in dreams, and revere them. "I had this dream the other night," we say, feeling certain that we are about to divulge some sacred truth. A coded message from God, if one believes in God. If we followed Hegel's thought, we'd probably be happier accepting dreams as truth, but we might also be lost, since it's been proved that we would prefer to live with lies, like tried-and-true history. The truth is, you reside in my mind, dead or alive, now and forever, in dreams and out, night and day, under the hide of me.

LAST NIGHT, when you weren't watching, when you were distracted by someone who had smashed a lightbulb on the kitchen floor linoleum, I entered your dream surreptitiously, in the disguise of a vicar, I believe, and observed the goings-on. Remember the Jack Yeats you liked, with the country people in the west of Ireland celebrating Saint John's Eve, tossing sods of paraffin-soaked turf in loops of fire, and Jack Yeats and Synge, standing in the background, very small and still, so small that you had to peer into the painting to notice them, just standing side by side, taking it all in? That was my place in your dream.

Your parents were there, unsurprisingly, though I had not remembered your father as being that tall, six-foot-six at least, and I did not recall that he wore brocaded vests, but he wore one there, ornate and delicate. I think it lit up, flickering red and green. And your mother, thin as sticks today, was fat in your dream, like a cookie jar cook, and she spoke like an ambulance siren. But this was your dream, after all. So I made no comment about the distortions therein. A cow was there, off to the side, black and white. And a wicker chair, which the cow disdained. And a polar bear, naturally, my constant companion. I hadn't noticed that he entered your dream with me. Just like him. Amy was there, too. I envied you. Even a dream is a dream.

I had no practice being in other's people's dreams. Of course, I know I have appeared in your dreams from time to time, because you told me so. But that was hearsay. This was on-the-scene reporting. And there you were aboard a Christmas sled, a little girl. I watched you swoop down a grassy hill, not snow, just grass that, upon closer inspection, turned out to be the hair on my head. I had become the boy with green hair, like that old movie with Dean Stockwell, antiwar, I think, the green hair symbolizing protest. And you were so small on your Christmas sled that you could slide down my head from that bump on the top to the nape of my neck.

Then you disappeared. I searched the landscape, which now was yellow and barren. But you had gone from your own dream, leaving me as its sole resident. You said, "Goodness is no name, and happiness is no dream." It seemed, then, that I had taken it over, lock, stock, and barrel. And all the details, the contents—the lock and the stock and the barrel, and the alarm clock with the shiny bell on the top, and the softball, and the navy yard—everything belonged to me. I did not know how to feel about that, because this was your dream I had entered surreptitiously, not my own, in which my head had played its oversize part. Then I heard something outside the dream, on the other side of it, as if on the other side of a bedsheet hung up to separate a room. It was you I heard. You had been distracted by someone who had smashed a lightbulb on the kitchen floor linoleum.

Go where you are loved, and where you love. But you, being you, will of course make the other choice, and head off for enemy quarters where you will be greeted by handshakes, chocolates, and flowers. There, people will tell you how splendid you look, how beautiful your mind is, while, out of your sight, they will plot your assassination. At night you sleep without dreams and curl a stupid smile on your stupid face.

As for those you love and who love you, you have persuaded yourself that they can wait. The remarkable thing is that they will.

Summer is the season for it. I dream and see the children when they were children, one at a time, standing on a lawn or on a playground, waiting for the ball to reach them. Their hug-me arms waver in the hot, wet air, as if they are attempting to embrace something vast and invisible. Their eyes blink away the sunlight. They stagger and stumble. It's hard to learn to play catch. In the beginning, you use your arms to cradle the ball against your chest; then you use both hands, then one. Soon you're shagging flies like Willie Mays and firing bullets sidearm like Robinson Canó, not having to think about the act.

They do not call it a game of throw, though throwing is half the bargain. The name of the game puts the burden on the one who receives, but there is really no game to it. Nobody wins or loses. You drop the ball, you pick it up. Once you've got the basics down, it doesn't matter if you bobble a ball or two, or if you can't peg it as far as you once could, or if you have to stare and squint to pick it out of the sky. Or so I tell myself as I groan out of a chaise in response to my son John's "Dad, wanna play catch?" He is our third, the last in a line of catch players. We stand about twenty yards apart. He gives me the better glove, and we begin. I loathe the leaden drag in my arm, the lack of steam in my throw. Live, I look like a slo-mo replay. Amazing I still can reach him.

He, of course, is a picture of careless and fluid engineering. He doesn't even look at the ball. It is just there in his hands, and then it's off again. We go back and forth in an essential gesture of sports. A ball travels between two people, each seeking a moment of understanding from the other, across the yard and the years. To play a game of catch is not like pitching to a batter. You do not throw to trick, confuse, or evade; playing catch, you want to be understood. The best part of the game is the silence, something underrated in the rearing of children. After the heartbreaking shootings in the schools, experts on TV say that parents generally ought to talk to their children more, which seems sensible enough. But they should also find situations in which talk is unnecessary, where they can tacitly acknowledge the mystery of their connection, and be grateful for it, in silent play. Nietzsche said there is nothing so serious as a child at play. He could have added, "or a grown-up either." I throw. John catches. He throws. I catch. The ball wobbles so slightly in the bright stillness that one can almost count the stiches.

A pitcher when I was thirteen, I threw my arm out, and my idiot coach said, "Pitch through the pain," and I did, and I was never able to throw hard after that. Maybe it was a bit of good luck. The advantage in later years, when I become a player of the game of catch, was that I was all motion and no speed—a change-up artist with nothing to change up on—so that the children could study the mechanics of throwing and anticipate making a catch without too much fear. Once I happened to be on the field at Yankee Stadium before game time when the players were warming up. Wade Boggs and Don Mattingly tossed a ball between them without a trace of effort, bodies rearing up and half-pivoting gently in a casual parody of a pitcher's full windup toward the plate. Every easy toss was delivered at a speed greater than a good high school fastball pitcher could generate. *Thwack, thwack, thwack* in the leather. And the silence between the men on the field. It was interesting to note that even at their level, this was still a game of catch.

We take what we get in our children, and do what we can with it, making compromises and adjustments where we are able, making rules and explanations, but for the most part letting things happen, come and go, back and forth. The trick, I think, is to recognize the moments when nothing needs to be said, as in other arenas of love. See John and me. The heat and silence of the day fit us like a glove. I toss the ball in looping arcs. He snaps it up as if waving it away, then tosses it back on a line, with much more on it. So we continue until our faces glow with sweat, and the sun drops, and we are touched by the shadows of the trees.

Boys are easier, so they say. And I suppose Carl and John were a little easier than Amy, who would pout for what seemed to me a month or two, and lose her temper from time to time, in part, we always felt, to show she had one. But the overriding truth was, we never had trouble with any of the children. I was more trouble than the three of them put together. They were good kids—good in school, good with us, with one another, with their friends. They were fun, funny, respectful, independent. Carl grew up to be a good husband to Wendy, a good wife. Amy, a good wife to her husband, Harris, also good. All became good parents. John will be good at these roles, too, once he gets round to marrying. Twelve years younger than Carl, nine years younger than Amy, he is in his midthirties now, and still, as the youngest, endures the uber-watching of his parents. When Amy died of an anomalous right coronary, undetected yet carried from birth, I asked the boys to get MRIs to determine if they had the same anomaly. Twenty-nine-year-old John said he'd go if I bought him a toy.

These days, the boys and I are together as a trio mainly for sports events—watching TV or occasionally at live games. We used to take baseball trips in the summers, following the Yankees on the road to Chicago, Toronto, Baltimore, and Kansas City. Each trip yielded memories associated with things outside the games—steaks and beer in Chicago; steaks, beer, and the Negro League Museum in Kansas City. At the Royals' Kauffman Stadium there was a kid hawking lemonade as he made his way through the crowd. His loud piercing sound: Lemonadelemonadelemonade! In Toronto, there was a big guy with a white beard, sitting on the aisle in the lower stands, who welcomed other fans and advertised himself as "Greeter Claus." The trips stopped when Amy died, but the three of us still gather to watch the Yankees, hobbled this season, the Jets, hopeless in any season, and, sometimes, the worthless Knicks. Amy was into sports, too, and a faster runner than either of her brothers. She became a game herself. After dinner Carl and John would announce that they were about to play the self-defining "Tackle Amy." The tacklee gave as good as she got.

Carl deals with government contracts at a big-money level. He maintains high positions because he's smart, thorough, and kind with people. At family get-togethers, he watches out for anyone sad or alone. John is like him in that. The funniest of our lot, he writes screenplays, and can imitate any foolish public figure with perfect pitch. He has a great ear for cant and bullshit. Amy, also deadpan funny, was a pediatrician. A careful parent, she would worry about her patients in the hands of the careless. All three became the kinds of grown-ups Ginny and I would have chosen for friends. Sometimes I sit back and watch the boys talking and standing together like construction workers on a break, their sister's ghost beside them.

"What do you call that house without walls?" says James from his perch behind me, in the car seat. I glance to my right. "It's called a gazebo, James," I tell him, "but I had never thought of it as a house without walls until you pointed it out." He thinks but says nothing, as he always does after receiving some piece of sought-after information. He takes in everything. I watch him in the rearview mirror. We are driving to his preschool.

"What do you call that building?" he asks. I tell him it's a church, a place where people gather to think about God. "What's that on the top?" I tell him about a steeple, that some steeples have bells inside them and some do not. The one we pass is too small for bells. "A steeple with no bells," he says.

We pass a small house. He asks if there is a name for such a house. I tell him that small houses are sometimes called cottages. He repeats the word. We pass another gazebo, where schoolchildren wait for their bus. He stares at the older, bigger children. "Gazebo," he says.

These daily drives to preschool have been our routine since Amy died when James was fourteen months. Now he is three. Sometimes we talk about things we see on the drive, sometimes about subjects that arise as a result of the things we see. One morning we passed a man replacing a flat with a spare. When told what the man was doing, James said he would like to invent something he called the Everything Car, which would be covered with spare tires, so that no one would ever be stuck or stranded.

All six grandchildren—Amy's Jessie, Sam, and James; Carl's Andrew, Ryan, and Nate—show their characters in their faces. Jessie, ironic and innocent; Sam, open; Andrew, determined; Ryan, exuberant; Nate, self-possessed. James's face is a mixture of the quizzical and contemplative. Harris took a picture of the back of his head as he watched fireworks on the Fourth of July. No one needed to see the face to recognize the subject.

"That's the shoulder of the road," he says, giving me back information he had picked up yesterday when he'd asked me what the road to the side of the highway was called. Now he asks what it is made of. I tell him I'm not certain. Asphalt, perhaps. I make a mental note to look it up, because James forgets nothing. He will ask me again. If I tell him that we'll work together on his Lego after school, he is not in the door five seconds before calling to me about our project. If I say, even tentatively, that we might make a trip to the Air and Space Museum, he dismisses the "might."

We are told that we make a pair, my pint-size grandson and me. Ginny showed me a photograph of me with my parents on vacation in Cape Cod when I was three. Same hair color, same smile. His hand is a small version of my own, a genetic replica. I tend to play mostly classical music in the car, which James absorbs, and occasionally expresses approval of, though generally he prefers Kelly Clarkson. He likes the name Bach, and repeats it frequently. "Is that Bach?" I gave him a Bach CD, and later found him tucked in a corner of the couch, listening to it on his earphones.

His older brother, Sammy, and I were watching him balance himself on the railing of a fence on the beach one summer day. James is remarkably strong and coordinated. He can climb a doorframe from the floor to the top, using only his hands and feet. He is also tough. When he takes a spill, he rarely cries, just shakes it off. "He never stops moving," I remarked to Sam, as we observed James's balance beam act. "He loves life," said Sam.

"What's that name?" I ask him as we pass a school called Saint James. "James!" he exults. Then he asks, "What's a saint?" "A very good person," I tell him. He thinks about that.

How much time do I have, do you reckon? It's a long long time from May to December, and the days started growing cold several years ago. In my mind, I mean. The body's okay, as seventy-three-year-old bodies go. But at this time of life it is only natural to calculate what remains (forget that I used "remains"), especially when one considers how one's light has been spent, mixing recrimination with desire. Time travels at different speeds over the long haul. Do you think that's why the Chinese ditched the clock? These days, my clock slows like someone walking in six feet of water (forget that I used "six feet"), or like someone quick-stepping past a traffic accident or a fire in a penthouse that then catches his attention, and he slows his pace to appease his curiosity. It helps to tell myself that I'm here for another decade, maybe two. That would be nice. I'd see the grandchildren grown. Get a little work done, if I keep my marbles. Best of all, if you'll walk with me, whatever our pace, I'll spend these precious days with you. These precious days I'll spend with you.

Saint Lucy told her mother, Eutychia, "Whatever you give away at death for the Lord's sake you give because you cannot take it with you. Give now, while you are healthy, whatever you intended to give away at your death." It was her way of saying, I imagine, that love is life and vice versa.

A redhead loiters at the counter in Paul Stuart, choosing a tie for her married lover. During the first two years of their affair, she refused his gifts. One time there was a gold chain, another an Hermès scarf. She would not get anything for him, either. Exchanges of gifts, she said, implied a more secure and respectable relationship than the one they were involved in. He said, Have it your way, though often he had wanted to get her things for her birthday, for Christmas, and especially for Valentine's Day. Now, after six years, her rules had relaxed, and today she is buying him a tie to celebrate one of his victories in business. "Are you getting this for your husband?" asks the salesclerk, a friendly young woman who is merely trying to be helpful. "Yes," says the redhead. "Does he prefer stripes, polka dots, or designs?" the salesclerk says. "Stripes usually," says the redhead, whose hair glows copperlike in the severe store lighting. "How long have you been married, if you don't mind my asking?" says the salesclerk. The redhead answers, "Six years," wishing that the conversation would come to an end. She takes the tie the salesclerk suggests. Soon she walks from Paul Stuart and boards the Madison Avenue bus uptown, with a box containing a very becoming blue-and-maroon striped tie tucked close to her side.

MADISON AVENUE IN THE FALL. Don't you love it? Autumn in New York. Don't you love it? The store windows. Paul Stuart's neckties, pink, green, yellow, and red. The antique vases. Sunglasses that stare at you as you walk by. Prints of noble dogs. Prints of ancient churches. *Prince of New York*. Such a movie. Such a city. Don't you love it? Gotta love it. Fifth, Lex, Park. NO PARKING. "Gay Yoga." And tell me, what street compares with Mott Street in July? Unless you're thinking of the Avenue, Fifth Avenue, where the photographers will snap us. I'll take Manhattan. I'm in a New York State of mind. NO STANDING. Gotta love it. Knockwurst, Sushi, Ethiopian. *The French Connection.* SIAMESE CONNECTION. The people ride in a hole in the ground. Tenements, what's left of them. Cobblestones, what's left of them. What's not to love? Let's stride to work on the Avenue of the Americas. Let's slouch home from work. Past the smells of horse carriages and bakeries. Guys sticking flyers in your face. Past the Hassids, and the Dominicans, and the big shots and Little Italy. Past the Korean grocers with the splurge of flowers out front: pink, green, yellow, and red. Love love love.

THEIR HEADS ARE BOWED at their desks like the flowers I have given them. This is an in-class writing assignment: write a page on what the flower smells like. It is an exercise in stream of consciousness for my students at the Southampton campus of Stony Brook University. The school is small and unadorned, spread out on a rise overlooking a bay; it is about to come in to flowers of its own in the reluctant spring thaw.

Write what it smells like. Go into the past. Follow your nose. This is what you will do as writers. You will plunder the past to explain the present and make the present more intense. Think of stream of consciousness as a detour off the path of the narrative. Go where it takes you, and when you get back, the main road will have changed. So they sniff, dream into the pictures their minds unearth, and write. A boy's hand is fixed to his forehead, covering one eye. A girl touches her lips with her pencil. They are all very still, separated from one another and from the classroom and the cold sun streaking in.

While they do their exercise, they become mine. Write what they look like: fifteen young people in jeans, sweatshirts, and sweaters, bodies hooked over a white sheet of paper, pursuing memories, dressing them up, and watching to ascertain that their hands are following their instructions. The flower is laid aside on the desk, its work done. The students are off now like hounds. They follow the scent to funerals, weddings, proms. One girl will remember lying in the night grass under a blue moon with her little sister. Another will recall a last dance with a midshipman in navy whites. A boy will alter the scent to that of lilacs, and swoop back to a childhood Eden near his father's rectory.

This is where education becomes private. This is the nub of it. It is out of sync with the conventional images of education in America. Write about those images: the teacher is a pale, bloodless deacon, drained by unrequited longings, preposterous, out of things. She is the withered maiden, he is Ichabod Crane, humiliated to death by the village nitwit. The only way he gains respect is to become

Glenn Ford in *Blackboard Jungle* and beat up the classroom hoods. There are exceptions like *Mr. Holland's Opus.* But the rule is Arnold in *Kindergarten Cop.*

For their part, students are depicted as at their most alive when they have as little to do with school as possible. Huck and Holden light out for their respective territories; Ferris Bueller is the god of glorious truancy. Or make an *Animal House,* and trash the joint. School is anticreativity, antifreedom, anti-American—an attitude only logically contradicted by a society that insists on higher education for all and accreditations up to the eyeballs.

Not that the derision is difficult to understand. Education is a setup for ridicule. Old people stuck in place deliver old information to new people about to move up and out. The adamant vs. the supple. The straitlaced vs. the unlaced, over whom they exert a flimsy and temporary authority. Every classroom is an implicit smirk. Write what you feel. Okay, I feel I am going to sit here and accept whatever that tired old bird dishes out, and then I'm going out on the green to toss a Frisbee, flirt, chomp on an Egg McMuffin, *live.* I'm going to leave him in his own dust. Meanwhile, the teacher, ever desperate to exhibit vital signs, forages for inspirational material. How to convey that this stuff is essential? How to get across that what is not practically useful is most useful? They are salmon in the springtime, and Professor Backward has one small porous net. To catch even one or two of these lovable fish. Is that worth a life, Mr. Chips? Fish and Chips?

I'm a half-time teacher, an amateur. It is the lifers who hold up the citadel, they who remain in the dusty stillness of the classrooms after the kids have tromped out. Amid the riot of *The Nutty Professor,* Eddie Murphy caught that look—all knowledgeable, all wistful, hopeless within his own superiority. Everything he makes vanishes except his monumental size. As he chalks one line of an equation on the blackboard, his belly erases the other line. He is a visual fat joke. But he has something to teach them. He takes them seriously.

"Take another minute to write. Then let's see what we've got."

They hunker down with their memories. Still so much to say. They have long ago left the smell of the flower behind and are taking the rapids. Their necks and shoulders are locked. Their hands are disembodied and skitter from left to right like the automatic returns on electric typewriters. Teaching is love, love teaching. One girl recalls her job selling roses at the side of the highway. Men stopped their cars to buy a bunch. She writes, "No one bought roses for me."

WHAT IS IT WITH YOU, that you can bring up the most obscure detail of something we did or said a hundred years ago, as a fitting annotation to whatever we're doing now? Are you a reference librarian? You seem to have memorized our lives. I will forage around: "Oh yes, uh, I think I remember that now." But you, you never forget a moment. Do you remember the reason why we married in the fall—to build a cozy nest, and to get a little rest. You are Mr. Memory in *The 39 Steps:* "The 39 Steps is an organization of spies . . . Am I right, sir?" Are you ever wrong?

Our domestic library is having its semicentennial this year. What do you think of that? I think I recall the first books we acquired for it. Or rather, you do. Now the place is growing obsolete along with its inhabitants, a house full of books when books are going out of style. We thought we were building a collection. Instead, an obselection. But the point is, you know it from head to distant tail. Do you use mnemonics to keep track of things? A Dewey decimal system? Who was Dewey, anyway?

I'm no you. The kind of shit I remember is Bob Grim's best pitching record on the Yankees (20–6), or the name of Samuel Johnson's cat (Hodge). But off the top of your sweet head you can recall the name of the people who let us try out their house in Vermont that winter weekend and of the guy from whom we rented that place in Truro in 1969, and how much it cost, and who was the babysitter we hired, and where she lived. So, here's my question: Since we seem to have lost ourselves again, and I can't make head or tail of this GPS, do you recall the way home?

Even when we fell apart, the sun remained a wafer in the sky, just like *The Red Badge of Courage.* Just like *The Red Badge of Courage,* I said. The pathetic fallacy, I said. You merely said pathetic, and walked away, disappearing part by part among the shoulders of the dunes. Yet nothing had changed in nature. The brows of the cliffs retained their hauteur. Trees were neither shorn nor shaken. Grasshoppers did their thing, as did polar bears somewhere, and gazelles somewhere else. The sea mocked time, as usual. Not one element of the universe regretted our calamity. In fact, if the Martian, who is often called upon to testify in situations such as this, had descended to observe the scene, he would have noticed nothing that was not accounted for in the handbook *America for Martians,* and nothing in the sky whence he had come, past the wafer and the unaltered positions of the stars. Save, perhaps, if he had looked a bit closer, using his interplanetary spectacles and his extraterrestrial vision, he might have picked up the slight fissures in the tree bark, and grasshopper tears.

This won't be worked out in bed, he tells her, who barely hears him, his back turned toward her. He is standing at the bedroom window, not looking at the night but seeming to. She asks him what he said. This will not be worked out in bed.

Where, then? she says. In the chem lab? On the stock

exchange? In the shrink's chair? Where, then? At the White House, where we may undergo an agonizing reappraisal? The lecture hall? The lecture hall, by all means, she says, where we can conjugate and decline. Our story is in declension. Or should we look at it as an enzyme that needs to be broken down? Or a frog, to be dissected on the floor beside the bed, where nothing will be worked out? The attack of the giant truisms: You do not love me. You love only yourself. And this old thing: What are you, a child? What am I, a child? he says, still turned away.

The silence of the Mediterranean coast is far away. The tender sea laps up against the shore where, naked, lovers lie. She's a broker. He's a nurse. They look to be on the verge of saying something stupendous, but just then a seagull wheels by and swipes the ham and brie sandwich from her hand. Surprised, they laugh. One of these days they will get around to marrying, but not today. We were never here. What *are* you?

In your lifeline, the fortune-teller says, I see a lyre and a cloud, construction paper, lilies and subaqueous tendencies. She explains nothing. She demands her money. What worries the woman who has just withdrawn her hand is not the symbology but rather why she sought out the fortune-teller in the first place. Now, like everyone else, she's stuck with mystifications. That night he says, what's eating you? Not you, she thinks. He has no clue. Evening makes us even.

This is the clavicle and this is the spleen. This is the early bird and this is the debt. This is the choke and this is the brake. This is the garden path. What's this? This is the slammer. The stammer. The clamor. Entwined in discord, we must extricate something of value from this experience, don't you think, she tells him, lest one morning I find myself holding your fresh skull in my hands, and declare too late that neither of us was a war criminal. By then, all I'll have to hold, to have and to hold, is your skull, and those dreadful letters and those dreadful pictures, in the album with the leatherette cover. Allow me to say, before we reach that point, that I am sick and tired of reproaches, more sick than tired. I drag my contaminated carcass to lie on stones in the creek.

Come, let us speak only of the New York mayoral race, which is heating up, and of Bosnian cuisine, and the price of wheat in Iowa. The summer of this union is stuck in a cellar door. Cobwebs. Cobwebs. Operator, give me the spider department.

Their folks were like this, and the folks of their folks, and so on into the mists of their family trees. In the tall dry grass he is six, and there is nothing but heat, bugs, and silence. One thing they agree on: If they continue down this road, no one will find them. Someone will jot down an entry in a log that the day they disappeared was the same day a red and blue hot air balloon vanished in the sky over Georgia, and the shrimp disappeared from the Gulf. What am I, a child? The conscience, too, can lie.

O tree and fruit. O song and dance. Face me.

IF I SIN AND STRAY, will you forgive me? For if that's what you have in mind—forgiveness—don't bother. I do not want your forgiveness. You do not want mine. Brenda Lee (remember her?) sang, "I'm sorry, so sorry. Please accept my apolo-gee." I'm sorry, too, Brenda. I don't. What's the point of forgiveness? If I take the Catholic rite of confession correctly, the however-many Hail Marys one is assigned are not supposed to let you off the hook for smoking in the library. It is meant to embrace the fact that you exist in the fold of human failing. If that is the case, then forgiveness means recognizing the whole sinner, not just dismissing the sin. That I do understand.

Let us forgive each other nothing. Would it not mean more if we agreed to indicate that sinning and straying are part of the human sonnet? Our song within limits? If you confess a sin to me, I will never forgive you. Not as long as you live.

WHAT WE TALK ABOUT when we talk about power. I mean real power, the force of suasion that enables one to issue orders and the other to follow them. The powerful people of history create a world of victories. I want no part of it. If we should create any world at all, let it be of ruins, of Yeats's rag-and-bone shop of the heart. From that shop, from that basement, debasement, one ascends only by acts of amnesty and appeasement. The power of the imagination is so much greater than the heroes of history, unless, as was the case with Lincoln, the imagination and the reconciliation are one.

If you take what is mine against my will, is that a show of power? Or (and naturally, all this is hypothetical) do I become the more powerful if I simply, gladly, give you what you want? I am happy not to resist you, to cede you power over me, for that gives me power over you. In a way, then—perverse, cunning—you are subject to the power of my powerlessness. The only trouble with such a formulation is that it makes a power game of love. And love is not that. Love is a work of the imagination. And imagination is funny. It makes a cloudy day sunny.

The point is not to back off if it starts to knock you about. That's just its way, uncivilized, like a food fight in a mess hall—cheeseburgers and spaghetti flying past each other under the lurid light of ancient college chandeliers. Why, you'll never get the place cleaned up. You'll run out of Lysol. And mops. And Fantastik. You'll run out of Fantastik. Why try? Think of the whole business as a lost cause from the start. Think of it as a splurge, a pig-out, or one of those buying sprees bipolar bears go on when they're in the manic stage. Eyes wild. Running from counter to counter in Macy's. Whoopee. You're a goner. You're a hat.

So what if you feel like jetsam. This is how you're supposed to feel. If I were you, I'd toss away your compass and your iPhone, and your car, while you're at it, and straddle the needle atop the Chrysler Building and jump, though killing yourself won't do much good. And you might land on someone valuable, as opposed to, say, you. Better to stomp from place to place like The Mummy, who, while an awkward son-of-a-bitch, at least had the advantage of carrying around his own bandages. Why don't you try singin' in the rain?

Or are we at that stage of it when the singin' in the rain is over, and so are the departing dance steps, and the puddle jumping, and we stand at the what-now after the cameras are turned off? Well, suck it up, pal. Love isn't a song, you know. Oh. You thought it was a song.

Early in his composing career, Cole Porter visited George Gershwin to ask his advice. Porter couldn't sell his songs. Gershwin told him to make them "more Jewish," meaning that Porter should include a greater number of minor chords to deepen the feeling toward sadness or melancholy. The results were "Night and Day," which goes minor in the third repetition of the first note; "The Still of the Night"; "Every Time We Say Goodbye" (noting "how strange the change from and major to minor"); and most everything else Porter wrote after consulting Gershwin. The lyrics and the minor chords work together to say, in effect, that the true philosophy of life, and love, consists of courage with resignation. The lover is wracked with doubt when he asks, "Do you love me as I love you? Are you my life to be, my dream come true?" Yet he asks the questions anyway, on the frail, brave hope that the answer will be yes.

Courage with resignation is the theme of Thomas Gray's "Elegy Written in a Country Church Yard," too. It's said that the poem is about disappointment, unrealized fame, and ambition—the flowers blushing unseen, the mute, inglorious Miltons buried in the obscure country cemetery. I don't think it's about disappointment at that level. I think the poem goes much wider and deeper, to praise the human courage to go on when, at the same time, one is resigned to failure. To such courage one pays "the tribute of a sigh." For it is not just the paths of glory that lead to the grave. Everything leads there. Knowing that, what should the noble life consist of but the courage to sing at the wall of defeat? We live at our best in a minor key, in the chill, still of the night.

On a green and gray-stone morning, when the trees look like shadows in a photograph, my thoughts all stray to you.

If those pushy mothers of the Plaza de Mayo, years ago in Argentina; if they would not go away no matter how the *policia* shoved them around; if they continued to walk up and down in front of the presidential Pink House carrying photographs on placards and holding snapshots between their index fingers and their thumbs; if they insisted day after day, sunshine or rain, that their children did indeed exist in spite of the fact that they had been "disappeared" by the thugs of the military government, and denied by their dogged persistence that there ever was such a thing as a *desaparecido*, or that anything beloved could vanish just like that . . . why would I think that you could ever disappear?

What we once enjoyed and deeply loved we can never lose, for all that we love deeply becomes a part of us.
—Helen Keller

Your official commencement speaker tackles the big themes, tells you to abjure greed, to play fair, to serve your community, to know thyself. Your more personally devoted commencement speaker agrees with all that. But he has special wishes for you, too—idiosyncratic, of course—what an educated daughter may have come to expect from an oddball father. People always said you resemble him.

What he wishes you first is a love of travel. Travel will hold you back from doting on your troubles, and once you've seen something of the world, you will recognize foreign places as instances of human range. The logic of Athens, the fortitude of London, the grace of Paris—a city for every facet of the mind. He would have you connect travel with an appreciation of the past as well. In Jerusalem, he walked the Old City, brushing thousands of years of faith and murder. He would like you to see yourself as history, to wonder what you would have shouted, or at whom, as Jesus struggled up the Via Dolorosa. He hopes that you will husband your own past, too. The past means possibility.

He also wishes you a love of animals, which you feel strongly already; he hopes that tenderness lasts and grows. Animals, too, draw people out of excessive self-interest, their existence a statement of need. A dog's eyes search your face for a mystery as deep as God, asking nothing and everything, the way that music operates. He hopes that you always love music, even the noisy boredom you clamp to your ears these days, while he harbors the prayer that in later years will follow Rachmaninoff and Bix Beiderbecke. If you learn to love jazz, you will have a perpetual source of joy at the ready. Jazz is *serious* joy, much like yourself.

For some reason, he has always favored culs-de-sac, so he hopes you live on one, someday, a neat little cutoff that surprises the city's motions with a pause. Trees on the street, he would like that for you. And low, modest houses so the sky is evident. He hopes that your mornings are stock still except for squirrels and birds, but that the evenings bulge with human outcry, families calling to one another in the darkening hours. He wishes you small particulars: a letter received indicating sudden affection, an exchange of wit with a total stranger, a moment of helpless hilarity, a flash of clarity, the anticipation of reading a detective thriller on a late afternoon in an electric storm.

He hopes that you learn to love work for its own sake. You have to be lucky for that (of course, he wishes you luck), and find a job that absorbs you and makes something useful of your curiosity. Something to do with helping others in your case, he should think, since he has seen your natural sympathy at work ever since your smallest childhood and has watched you reach toward your friends with straightforward kindness. Friends, he knows, you will have in abundance. He wishes them *you*.

Eccentrics: He hopes that you always have plenty of them about you, and few, if any, sound thinkers. Sound thinkers appear on television; academies award them

your weight class, always fight up. Hatred without a fight is self-consuming, and fighting without hatred is purposeless, so regretfully he wishes you some hatred, too. But not much, and not to hold too long. There is always more cheapness in the world than you suspect, but less than you believe at the time it touches you. Just don't let the trash build up. And there is much to praise.

In general, he wishes that you see the world generously, that you take note of and rail against all the violence and the want, but that you also rear back and bless the whole. This is not as hard to do as it may seem. Concentrate on details, and embrace what you fear. The trick is to love the world as it is, the way a father loves a daughter, helpless and attached as he watches her stretch, bloom, rise past his tutelage to her independent, miraculous ascendancy. But you must never let go entirely, as he will never let you go. You gave birth to each other, and you commence together. Good-bye, my girl.

IF LOVE IS THE MOST POWERFUL and insistent force in the world . . .

Who said it was? [Argumentative]

If love is the most powerful and insistent force, if love makes the world go round . . .

Enough. [Annoyed]

. . . Then why is there so much killing?

Really want to know? The answer is simple. It's your fault.

[Expressions of shock, irritation, and incredulity]

It's your fault. [Points to audience] See that fellow over there? The pleasant-looking bald guy in the beige sweater and jeans?

[Looks] I see him.

Why don't you go and sit beside him, introduce yourself, strike up a conversation, invite him over to your place for a meal, watch a movie or a ball game with him, and find out if there's any way you can be of help to him, anything he needs?

But he's a stranger.

[Sighs.]

He was too old and she was too young and it was too late and the snow was too heavy and they were too cold. So they huddled together on the floor near the fire, lying shoulder to shoulder and thigh to thigh. Each was too quiet. How they had wound up in the cabin, no one knows. He knew too many things. She knew too few. But they loved each other. And that was too bad.

Not that they ever had touched, until that night in the cabin. Not that they did more than touch there either, shoulder to shoulder and thigh to thigh. They would not even have been in that position, had the snow not fallen too fast, socking them in. They had lit a fire that was not too hot. And he told her, You are too beautiful. And she listened with a heart that beat too fast. And when the snow got to be too great, and the temperature inside the cabin too low, they lay side by side on the floor, which was not too hard, each thinking too much.

IN ANCIENT EGYPT, a trial period to determine whether or not a marriage was working included not only an assessment of how good the couple were in bed, but also took into account how they were at the dinner table. Compatibility in love of food was as important as compatibility in lovemaking. I read this in James and Kay Salter's *Life Is Meals*. The Egyptians called their trial period "a year of eating," and if dining with each other did not work out as well as dining on each other, the couple split. There was common sense to this practice. No two people have ever been so in love as to spend nearly as much time screwing as eating.

I'm no gourmet, but I know a few, as well as some cooks whose amorous passion for food is so fiery and beautiful, it makes one appreciate eating as an art. Dan Halpern, poet and editor, loves great food, and creates it. Some years ago, he gave us a two-volume edition of *elBulli, 2004*, displaying photographs of foods so arresting one easily could mistake them for paintings. Mango, pistachio, and yuzu peel cup. Hot duck foie gras jelly with green barley couscous in argan oil. Nopal with prickly pears. One dive into these books, and there is no mystery as to why one falls in love with food, or why so many terms of endearment—cookie, honey, apple dumpling, sugar, cupcake—are delicious. A hundred and one pounds of fun, that's my little Honeybun. You're the apple of my eye, sweet Adeline. You're a peach. Peaches came from China, by the way.

My taste in food runs cheap, to burgers, pasta, fries, and ice cream. When I say that I love such stuff, I'm not kidding. I love it. I even associate romantic love with certain foods, such as Reese's Peanut Butter Cups, which brought about my first taste of love, brief but memorable.

One Saturday, when I was eleven or twelve, I went to the Academy of Music movie theater on Fourteenth Street not far from my neighborhood of Gramercy Park. Before the movie started, I surveyed the candy counter, and thought I would try Reese's for the first time. I liked chocolate and peanut butter independent of each other, so I reasoned that I'd like the ingredients combined.

Just as I was taking my first bite of the scrumptious little pie, a girl my age sidled up to me at the counter. I recognized her as one of the girls who hung around the street gangs on Third Avenue. She had long reddish hair, and wore jeans and a sweatshirt. I thought she looked like Rita Hayworth. She said, I'm Carmen. Then she said, You're cute. Then she walked away. No girl ever had said anything even vaguely romantic to me before. I took another bite of my Reese's. Had Carmen and I lived in ancient Egypt, we might have married. And since I had no idea at that age of what one was supposed to do in bed, we could just have had lots of meals together—staring at each other across the dinner table, I eating Reese's, she whatever she liked.

"DELICIOUS, ISN'T SHE." Oleg Kitchen sighs as he observes his wife from his perch atop the wicker stool beside the garlic press, his celery green Marimekko trousers and tie-dyed T-shirt lending him the appearance of a young Greek sailor more than that of the fifty-five-year-old chief of psychiatric services he is or, rather, was, until he "chucked it all" for the "very special, very private" life now shared with Frigga Kitchen. She, doused in sunshine from the kitchen skylight, hums a Finnish folk song as she beheads a red snapper—"You cannot find this outside the Bahia"—in preparation for the evening's *peixada*. [This is the eighth in our series, "Love Eats, Love Self."] "The kitchen is our life," Oleg continues. "All we have is here."

Which, from the looks of some eight hundred square feet of polished blond wood floors and tables, the blond wood jars and spoons, the blond wood butcher blocks and blond wood beams, from which hangs "perhaps the most comprehensive aspic mold collection in the East," is plenty. "We make our own napkins," adds Frigga. "And our own salt." She has gracefully sidled over to a bowl marked ZUPPA INGLESE. Her hair, the color of blond wood, is garnished with a sprig of thyme.

This remarkable kitchen constitutes nearly the entire house of the Kitchens, who have "ruthlessly brushed aside" the original walls of their eighteenth-century saltbox to make room for what they call "our shrine to cooking, eating, loving, and mutual respect." No longer regarding the living room as the center of the home, they have simply done away with it, as they also have done away with a library and even a dining room. "They are not separate things, the preparation and consumption," Oleg states emphatically, barely missing the Salton yogurt maker with his fist. "Why have separate places for them? As for the living room"—he gestures expansively with a paring knife as he starts to stuff the *tufoli*—"that was the old life" [a veiled reference, we believe, to his six former marriages]. "This is freedom."

"And honesty," Frigga adds quietly, leafing through her copy of *Cold Cuts of the Arctic*. [We nod and smile.]

"Honesty above all," Oleg agrees, tenderly lowering a deveined shrimp into the mouth of the former Finnair hostess and industrial spy.

The Kitchens have made their new home in the heart of sumptuous Kitchen Synchs, the recently developed "total community" near Rye, New York. Everyone within the community is recently remarried—"reborn really,"

Oleg tells us; is also a gourmet chef; and has been the subject of at least one life-at-home article in a newspaper or magazine like ours. The residents take great pride in their kitchens, and make a point of dropping in on one another once or twice a day to compliment some goody simmering on the stove. As we are admiring the Belgian wire whisk that Frigga swears was once the property of Paul Bocuse, a neighboring couple, Art and Haute Cuisine, who look astonishingly like the Kitchens themselves, stop by in tears to report the theft of a pair of tarragon driers they had lucked into in Barcelona. And there is much saddened head shaking over the fact that theft is not unknown in Kitchen Synchs.

"You see," Frigga, shaken, but not stirred, explains after the Cuisines have departed, "there is nothing else of real value in a place like this. To us the kitchen is not merely functional; it is [here she flounders in Finnish until Oleg provides "spiritual"]. Exactly so," Frigga continues, "spiritual. That is why Oleg and I do everything in the kitchen, why we rarely leave, for any reason." [At that we chuckle, and ask teasingly if they make love in the kitchen, too.]

"But of course," they answer as one, to our delighted surprise. Oleg indicates several bright pots scattered on hot trays about the room. "Some of these dishes take days to prepare. You don't want to let them out of your sight for a minute. We've mastered the art of making love while never taking our eyes off our Wolf double oven," he adds, acknowledging our light applause.

Yet Frigga shakes an apple corer scoldingly at her husband. "Tell the truth, Oleg, It's not because we really need to watch the pots that we live in the kitchen. It's because we love the kitchen. The kitchen is love. Is that not so?" Says Frigga, "All we need is love . . . and paprika." Whereupon Oleg hurls aside the colander, nearly toppling La Machine, and sweeps his wife into his arms, as if she were a freshly baked scone. "You are right, my beet, as usual," he says. And they do a little two-step, which they call the dance of the shucked oysters, leaving us to wonder aloud if such a pair could ever become bored.

"Bored?" asks Oleg.

"Bored?" asks Frigga.

[They laugh like sparkling water from the center of the earth.]

It's a put-down to think of a woman in the kitchen these days. He understands. Yet when he is away, briefly or for a week or two—driving, sitting in a plane, or in a piano bar—that is where he pictures her. He sees her back as she faces the kitchen counter, chopping or washing. Chopping celery or washing apples. Or kneading dough like a memory, or standing at the stove, stirring some thick concoction where the flames lick the bottom of the pot. He cannot make out what she is doing, exactly, only her back and shoulders responding to the deft movements of her hands. What wouldn't he give to be as good at anything as she is at these tasks, which seem, for her, automatic. The workings of the virtuoso. She is humming "You Are My Lucky Star." The recessed ceiling lights dazzle the curls in her hair, running up and down her curls like the lights in a pinball. She could be anywhere. A cornfield. A ship. The dinner plate in her hands might be a ship's wheel.

If he could paint, he would paint her, over and over, the way painters do. A version here, another version there, never quite getting it right. In art, one strives for the nature of things, but the nature of things will not be tamed. Could he ever re-create her? He thinks of Elsa Lanchester in *The Bride of Frankenstein,* before she made those herky-jerky movements of her head. What life could he breathe into his bride? What hairdo could he give her? Not Elsa Lanchester's, for sure. He tires of self-recrimination, self-observation, self. The same old punishments for going down for any sailor who whistles at him. But she. She's another matter. She's another matter altogether.

In Vermont some years ago, he'd observed a sheep caught in a bramble bush on a hill above a stream. It was winter. The stream was frozen. The sheep struggled against the brambles. It panicked and bleated. He'd started down the hill to try to help the thing and free it, but with each approaching step of his, the animal panicked more, and the bleating grew louder. So he backed off, understanding that sheep do this. They get caught in bramble bushes, and they work things out on their own. Or they don't, and they die. That is their nature.

She is doing something he cannot see. He sees only her back, as if she were a magician who has turned away from the audience for a moment to create an act of legerdemain, which, when she turns back will result in gasps and applause. Above her head, the kitchen window shows the knowing face of the moon, which alone beholds the potatoes and the peeler.

Paul Tillich's mother used to tie a rope around him when he was a toddler, and fasten it to a point in the center of the kitchen. The kitchen was where she spent most of her time, so she wanted to be sure that her baby theologian toddled in a safe place. Being German, she also attached a bit of discipline and moral purpose to her rope, which allowed little Paul to wander anywhere within the confines of the kitchen, but no farther. He was able to look into the dining room, for instance, but not able to go there. He saw what he could not reach, and had to restrict his adventurous imagination to a proscribed space. For the future theologian, this made the kitchen a sort of Eden. Like Eden's two principal residents, he could enjoy where he was but not where he wanted to be. Mrs. Tillich's lesson, like God's, one supposes, is that life has limits, and one had better make the most of them.

Well, I'm no theologian, baby. And I don't use ropes. But this bed has limits. Do you see where I'm going with this?

Seeing's as how the two teenagers don't have the scratch for a motel, much less a hotel, yo; seeing's as how there's no motel or hotel around here anyway, yo; and the woods are atingle with mosquitoes, and the field behind the shed is steeped in mud, which is messed up, yo, they turn their explorers' eyes to the dozen or so antique cars parked in the lot and awaiting the antique cars show tomorrow morning. But seeing's how this still is night, yo, and no one at the beach is standing guard over the cars in the parking lot, and most everyone's attention is focused on an R&B band playing "Kisses Sweeter Than Wine" under a tent, the two of them saunter among the Flivvers and Model T's, and settle upon a 1923 Duesenberg, with mahogany detailing and brown leather seats, into the backseat of which they tumble, strip, and fuck like bunnies, yo.

If, in my sleep, I shout unintelligible names or indicate anguish in a garbled tongue, or speak of Paul Tillich's mother, or of light as the shadow of God, or of polar bears or Chinese clocks, or of people made of bark and Kleenex, or utter a lament in Spanish, though I do not know Spanish, or laugh—laugh wildly—you may be sure that I am dreaming of a black glass wall with tall, cracked ladders leaning against it, and I am clambering up the side, only to find that I am crawling on the ceiling of a tunnel, and below me are red horses in stampede—dreaming, that is, of my life as an impossible puzzle.

So please do not push or nudge or tap or make an effort to get me up, for I fear that I may wake into sleep, and understand everything.

DREAM LOVER, whenever I want you all I have to do is dream. The way you haunt my dreams. Will you dream a little dream of me, too? An impossible dream, my dream operator? Like Thelonious Monk's dream. Or John Lennon's. Sweet dreams. California dreaming. I can dream, can't I? With my eyes wide open I'm dreaming on a star, down the boulevard of broken dreams, big city dreams. This time the dream's on me. I'll be home for Christmas, if only in my dreams. And you can tell me I'm not dreaming when I get you out of my dream and into my car, my beautiful dreamer, my sweet dream baby. Mr. Sandman, send me a dream. I mean, you got to have a dream, or how are you going to make a dream come true?

Sing me a song of scholarship.

That's not a song.

Sing me a song of the Greeks; of *philia, eros, agape, storge,* and *xenia*.

They all mean love. Right?

Yes. Sing me a song of the scholarship of love.

Love personal or love universal?

Both. Let us cover the entire subject, the entire canon, the oeuvre. From the Chinese philosopher Mozi, who said we should love all people equally, to the Persian *eshgh,* derived from the Arabic *ishq*, meaning "all-encompassing love," to the Turkish *ask,* which refers to the love of one person alone.

Ask me how do I feel, little me with my dead quiet upbringing.

Very funny. Perhaps we should simply focus on the Apostle Paul, in 1 Corinthians—"Love is patient, love is kind. It does not envy, it does not . . ."

Yes, yes. By all means. Let us focus on the Apostle Paul. But first, let us sing, "Don't know much about history. Don't know much biology."

You seem impatient.

More than you know.

Sing me a song of the scholarship of love.

That's not a song.

You see, a sigh is just a sigh. And that's saying something, because who knows what a sigh is? The word seems to have entered the language in 1300 as a form of the Old English *sighte,* perhaps as echoic of the sound it makes. Or around the same time as the word *swoon* or *suowne,* meaning "a state of unconsciousness," probably from the Old English *aswogan,* meaning "to choke," or the Low German *swogan,* meaning "to sigh." In the late fourteenth century came the verb *sough,* meaning "to make a moaning or murmuring sound." The verb *suspire,* in the mid-fifteenth century, came from the Latin *suspirare*—"to draw a deep breath." To *conspire* means literally to "breathe together." In *Romeo and Juliet,* Shakespeare gives us, "Love is a smoke raised with the fume of sighs." And, there's Gray again—"the tribute of a sigh."

With all that, a sigh is still just a sigh. No one has researched the word completely, and no one understands it. A questionnaire study revealed that most people associate sighing with sadness, or a resignation to sadness, or with futility. But that seems too easy for something everyone does again and again in a lifetime. Even laughter, another mysterious human sound, excites more thoughtful analyses from thinkers like Henri Bergson, who said we laugh because of the breaking of fluidity or momentum. One sighs from boredom, disappointment, frustration, weariness, and irritation. One sighs in love.

And see how harmless, how unthreatening is the

sound, certainly as compared to laughter, which can make the bang of a weapon. A sigh may be at once the most emotionally complex and timid sound we make. And the most private. The gentle breath one offers to fate. So difficult is it to define that it may be interpreted in several ways at the same time, only one of which is accurate, as its meaning belongs solely to the one who sighs.

The song ranks it among the "fundamental things," like a kiss. So a sigh, being fundamental, may not mean but be. A sound full of feeling, perhaps full of more feelings than anything we ever say, saying more than we are able to say, or even sigh. More than we know.

You see, a kiss is still a kiss. Philematology, the study of kissing, hasn't yielded much information on this subject, either, though one of the scholars who looked into it was Darwin. The word comes from the Old English *cyssan*, which became *coss*. One of the earliest descriptions of this delightful form of mouth-to-mouth resuscitation occurs in the *Song of Songs,* in the Old Testament—"May he kiss me with the kisses of his mouth / Because his lovemaking is better than wine." Jimmie Rodgers. "Kisses Sweeter Than Wine." Otherwise, there isn't a great deal of recorded history.

It isn't practiced everywhere, at least as a kiss involves the lips. Before the twentieth century, the Japanese simply didn't do it. Lithuanians and Letts did it. But not the Japanese. Neither did Africans. It was common in ancient Greece and Rome. In China, a different sign of affection was offered by rubbing one's nose against the cheek of another. In Southeast Asia, they have the "sniff kiss." On-screen kissing has been banned in India since the 1990s, and in Muslim countries, a man who kisses a woman not his wife may be put to death. Religions use it. The kissing of a pope's foot or a bishop's ring. The kissing of a prayer book or the Torah. Only in America, as the saying goes, has kissing flourished as an open expression of love, though it ranks second to hand-holding as the most frequently demonstrated form of physical intimacy. I wonder who was counting.

How did it come to be one of the fundamental things? One theory holds that it derived from mothers kissing infants, but it's a long way from that gentle expression to the passionate kiss of a Rudolph Valentino, or the record set on Valentine's Day 2013, when a couple from Bangkok held a kiss for fifty-eight hours, thirty-five minutes, and fifty-eight seconds. As for scholarly analyses, there is even less to say about a kiss than a sigh. We are here, you and I. Maybe millions of people pass by. So, kiss me while the world about us shatters. How little it matters, how little we know.

A KISS, A SIGH, and you and I went for a walk. Let's go. But because this excursion is monumentally important, should we not first go for supplies? Like Tonto? Head to the feed store or the general store or Bloomingdale's, and gather up all the stuff we will need? Tell me more about this trip of ours. Just the going was a cause for celebration, you said, and I'll buy that. I'm game. Yet something in (ornery, pig-headed) me wants to address the issues. Sleep with me, you said. We'll figure out the itinerary. You were right.

This excursion. It's about us, isn't it? It's about making our way over the swales of the dunes to the weir, then swimming out, faithful to the water. Research shows that couples do better on land. Yet out we go on this undulation, while lined up on the shore centuries of sentries cluck and cavil. (Did I write that?)

Think of our going as a returning, you said. And you were right. Think of it as a returning, the way Greek epic heroes return, or turtles to their birthplace in Mexico, or the Chinese to their clock. There will be plenty of time for toasts and carpentry later, when the two of us begin to crack like frost. Forget the supplies. Forget everything. No amount of preparation can equal ships leaning together, as the world takes under advisement the reckless silliness of us.

You are the only reason for the creek. And the red barn. You are the only reason for that. And the hullabaloo, and the donnybrook, and the fracas. Geometry. Medieval monks. Brown pears. You are the only reason for them as well. The black notes on the piano. The bell that gonged in a church in Vermont. The risks I take from time to time. The lift of the Dead Sea. The baby's breath (not the flower). Same. Makes one wonder where the world would go without you. To some dark mythical hell, I imagine, a rental storage locker, and all that was left would echo like an empty gym. You are the only reason the inky-dinky spider goes up the waterspout, creeps to the porch, broad jumps to the swing, and sings its heart out.

What if I were to go missing, as they say these days—go missing, and become a missing person—what would you tell the police? Wait. Before we get into that, let us consider how difficult it is for anyone to go missing. Now, especially, with iPhones and iPads and tweets and twitters and the other devices that make it compulsive to stay in touch. Even in the old days, with disappearing acts like Judge Crater, Amelia Earhart, D. B. Cooper, and Jimmy Hoffa, vanishing without a trace was thought so impossible, those who did it achieved the stature of folk heroes. It is amazing that anyone disappears, ever. Please don't talk about me when I'm gone.

All that aside, what would you say to the police to better enable them to search for me? Give them my height, weight, the color of my eyes? A recent photograph would help. An inventory of my hobbies, preferences in food, and clothing. Or would you simply tell them my routine, how I'm devoted to you night and day, sunrise, sunset, which fact, when you come to think of it, would offer a clue to my disappearance, since I never would leave you voluntarily. He must be kidnapped, you might say. Or the victim of an accident. Let's check the hospitals. He never would go missing on his own.

But do not concern yourself with this contrivance. I am not missing. I am where you know I am, always, where you can count on me to be. Somewhere, writing.

FOUR THINGS TO LEARN about writing. First, learn to love plain speaking. Build a bear, the way the kids do, from the straightforward bear outward to the adorned. But initially concentrate on the bear qua bear. A hat will look awkward on his head unless the head is right. Give him no bear shoes, until you have the feet down cold. (Do polar bears get cold feet?) The point is not just to keep it simple, but to appreciate the simple, and to love it for what it is. The bear. The noun. The thing. There is nothing like a bear, nothing in the world.

Second, learn to love right action. Summon your bear to a land where the weak are tormented by the strong. Call upon him to defend the weak and the good. Too easy? Never. That shows how little you know of life. Nothing is more difficult, or more important, than to defend the weak again the Evil One. Nothing is more difficult than to pursue truth, either. Let your bear do that. Let him ascend a mountain. Yes, call it Bear Mountain. He has no idea what awaits him at the top. So the bear goes over the mountain to see what he can see.

Third, learn to love the rules so that you can break them, so that you can show them how much you love them by breaking them. Bears break rules all the time—unruly bears—especially when they're in love. What are the lines from that Portuguese song (is it Portuguese?)? "You say my music goes against the rules, but rules were never made by lovesick fools."

Fourth, learn to love everybody, including the Evil One, and those who beat up on the weak. Love them, too. Put your bear in their place, so that he understands how they tick. Writing makes sorrow endurable, evil intelligible, justice desirable, and love possible. I wrote that somewhere before, too. I shall do it again and again. And love possible. Feel love stirring in your bear, until he stands atop his mountain, all seven feet of him, roaring, paws raised in triumphant understanding. Oh, my bear.

TWO MORE THINGS TO LEARN to love about writing: the work itself and where it goes. On the work itself? Swonderful, smarvelous, and as often as not, sroyal pain. Smuch for that. On where it goes?

Years ago, I wrote a story for *Time* on "Children of War," about kids in war zones throughout the world, and what they were thinking. In the Ka Wi Dang refugee camp in Thailand, I spoke with Seng Ty, who was an eight-year-old at the time. He had escaped from one of Pol Pot's child slave labor work camps, after having buried his parents with his hands. His mother had died of starvation. His father, a doctor, was executed by firing squad because he was educated, wore glasses, and thus was deemed an enemy of the state. A couple in Massachusetts read the *Time* piece and adopted Seng Ty, to rear as their own. Now he is American, married, has kids, and works to help Cambodian refugees here. We write each other. He comes to visit.

A few months ago, I received a call from the mother of a seven-year-old girl who was murdered in the Sandy Hook school massacre in Connecticut. The woman had read *Making Toast* and *Kayak Morning,* about Amy's death in 2008. She told me the books had helped her in her grief. Her daughter had wanted her family to have a house by the sea, so now they plan to move and live by the sea. Later, she sent me a letter, containing the program of a church service for her daughter, and a photograph of their little girl, which I placed beside a picture of Amy on my writing desk.

Often, at that desk, I am so completely submerged in whatever I am writing that I lose track of everything, get frustrated, clasp my head in my hands, and wonder why anyone would do this sort of work. Then I look up.

More than you know. This life. The way it tunes the mind. The other day, my wrist locked in a writer's cramp at the moment I was Googling ancient Greece. Google gave me everything about ancient Greece except ancient Greece. What about the bleached fields and the wild dogs? I thought. Not one mention of the wild dogs, starving, loping about the bleached fields, or about the potato pits, or the pikes after the battles had quieted, and the dead soldiers lying in the bleached fields. Nothing about the wild dogs eating the bodies of the soldiers, chewing on the bones, or about the pikes turned brown with hardened blood. Not a word. Not a single entry began: While the dogs were eating their husbands, the wives of the soldiers stood at the doors of their cottages, searching the horizon for a flash of spear in the sunlight. Ah, Google. Were these things not as much a part of ancient Greece as Sophocles or Pericles? Ah, Google, who has all the world's knowledge within thy grasp. What about the dogs and their bloody mouths?

This life. This window. This tree. This way of thinking. This tree rubbed with wax and glowing like an astronaut. More than you'll ever know.

On a weekend for which a light dusting was forecast, a good four inches fell on Quogue. They wouldn't call four inches snow in places like Butte and Fargo, but on the southern shore of eastern Long Island the amount is impressive. It makes a sudden New England of an area that, in fact, was settled before most of New England, in the mid-seventeenth century. The steep roofs of the New England–like houses are lathered with snow, and the surprisingly tall pines are shagged with ice, the way they get in Vermont. The main difference is the beach. There is snow on the beach.

I walk there on a Sunday morning. The snow draws a wide lateral strip at the top, and where it stops, the sand, brown and wet, continues to the lip of the ocean. I suppose the tide washing ashore made that portion of the sand too warm and moist to sustain the covering of snow, so half the beach is snow and the other half sand.

Sights like this are jarring to the senses because our experience tells us that certain things, both in and out of nature, do not belong together. Méret Oppenheim's fur-covered cup, saucer, and spoon is always upsetting, no matter how often one looks at it, because we tend to keep certain textures and functions segregated in our minds. Snow on a beach is not upsetting in the same way, but it startles the imagination. Where a child built a castle in the sand, he might make a snow fort in winter. My mind drifts in this direction because, no matter that I know there is no reason for bringing the snow and the sand together in an intelligible whole, still, one is always trying to connect disparate things. How should one drink tea out of an animal? What can I make of snow on a beach? Why was George with Gracie? Why are *you* with *me*?

Students of my generation were taught that E. M. Forster's dictum "only connect" is a prescription for the moral life. It was assumed that making connections was a sign of the mind's worth and purpose. Only connect; things fall apart; these fragments I have shored against my ruins. Perhaps this effort to bridge and yoke was a consequence of the big bad Bomb, and of a world growing up under the persistent threat of disintegration. Perhaps it was simply an invention of the academy in which exam questions insisted on one's making sense of this as related to that. We are naturally antianarchic, prounion.

Some years ago, I was watching the Academy Awards on one channel, staring at the shimmering people. And then I flipped to another channel where the news was showing some eighty dead bodies swaddled in body bags on the floor of an auditorium. They were the victims of the Happy Land social club fire in the Bronx. Flip: the Academy Awards. Flip: the dead of the Bronx. I wondered how these things fit together in the world. Would there be a movie made of the Happy Land fire? Would it win an Oscar?

So I sympathize with people who seek to create a

unity of thought and emotion out of disorder, but I also believe that trying to fit parts into a whole makes each component smaller, less interesting, and inauthentic. There is a life of parts as valid as the life of the whole. Simply noting is often enough. What right have I to give the universe a shape other than the one in which it presents itself without comment? The world steps forward as Dennis Rodman more often than as Grant Hill, bad as it wants to be, still loco after all these years.

The sad truth (Is it sad?) is that no great story ever makes sense, nothing important is to be understood, and no part fits. Homer was blind, Beethoven deaf. Blake's wife couldn't read. And I am that stumblebum on the beach, loving you.

AT HOME, the piano bar player has a Yamaha keyboard. The brightness of the sound, the action of the keys are as good as most Steinways. Using the wobbly loud pedal feels a little clumsy, but it's no big deal. He loves his Yamaha. At night, when the woman who came into his piano bar those many years ago, and with whom he has been sharing a lifetime since—when she is asleep upstairs, he will go to his keyboard and play this and that, whatever comes to his fingers. All these years, he really has not improved much. He still can't read music, and he hasn't added a great deal to his repertoire. He likes the old songs, the standards.

Right now, he's playing "Call Me," but he doesn't know the bridge, so he makes it up. He does that a lot with the bridges of certain songs. And when they call for key shifts that prove too difficult for him, he keeps the key he has been playing in. Who, after all, is going to tell?

Once in a while he'll play a tune perfectly, which in his terms means as good as it was written, even better, though, of course, he's faking it. Only the other night he was playing "Someone to Watch Over Me," when out of nowhere came the idea to hit F sharp at irregular intervals, as if someone outside were tapping at the window of the song. So pleased was he with the effect of this inspiration that he played the tune three times without pausing. He wanted to remember what he was doing, so that he could play "Someone to Watch Over Me" his special way after that. Either the song or his addition to it awakened his love, for there she stood behind him, watching over his shoulder as she had done that first night in the piano bar. That's new, she said, indicating the irregular F sharp. Once in a while, babe, he said, something new.

How crazy is this? I would like to remember you at the same time as I experience you, now. Let me rephrase that. I would like to live in the memory of you, but also in the present, so that there would be no distinction between my knowing the you you are and recalling the you you would become, later. What I mean to say is, I would like to remember you exactly as I know you, because I never want my memory of you to be different (better, worse, it matters not) than my current certain knowledge of you. You know how memory can be—distorting, exaggerating, concealing. Well, I don't want that.

But, how certain are you of your current knowledge of me? you ask. How can you be sure that you are not creating, distorting, exaggerating, concealing memories of me in the present, you ask, as you go along, like rapid-fire war photographers, *clickclickclickclickclick*? And I reply, pathetic as ever, I don't. I do not know about that. What I do know is that I simply want to love you in the future as I love you in the past. And to do that, I must remember you in the present. And you say, Call that simple?

Now the stars crisscross like lanterns swung at the tail end of a caboose. I, too, swing on my porch. Through my fancy new Dr. Dre headphones, riding my head like a jockey, roars Tony Bennett and Lady Gaga belting "The Lady Is a Tramp" in such cool fullness, it blows my mind. Blows my mind. At last I understand the phrase. We were never closer.

Know why the Chinese forgot they invented the clock? They did it deliberately. Like you, they wanted something to believe in here and now, the empire, the world before their very eyes. They wanted to live where subatomic particles collide at random. Stick a clock in a room, and the room revolves around time. Remove the clock, and everything coalesces at once, then separates, then coalesces again, and again, boom, in the same place. If each cell has a soul, then we have millions of souls. Think of that. And who knows if you were meant for me, or I was meant for you? The absence of time creates the presence of faith, and we are bedlam, darling.

THE STORY I HAVE TO TELL is of you. Of others, too. Other people, other things. But mainly of you. It begins and ends with you. It always comes back to you.

OURS IS A SUMMER VILLAGE, and it is unusual to see lights in the houses after the fall has come and gone. But on this winter weekend, perhaps because of the new snow, people have come back, and the windows of the houses blaze. I am accustomed to walking the length of the street after dinner in near total darkness, so it makes for a happy surprise, this startled brightening. In the dead black cold of night, the windows seem to ripple with gold and amber assertions of the light. The moon turns its knowing face. I know. I told you that already. Stay with me.

Of course, I really could be anywhere, at anytime. I could be a traveler in nineteenth-century Russia, for instance, tromping from village to village on some unspecified romantic errand, crushing the thick-caked snow under my boots, and taking courage from the lights of the candles in the cottages. Winter lights have much the same power the world over.

I recommend to you an essay by Virginia Woolf about the magical hours of the winter days in London, when the sky dropped like a velvet drape, and the streetlamps and the lights in the shops popped on in protest.

I also recommend a biography of Thomas Edison by Neil Baldwin, which contains a description of the winter night when Edison put his invention on public display. At his home in Menlo Park, New Jersey, he created the world's first showplace for electric light. Crowds of reporters and others would trudge up a hill to see lampposts set fifty feet apart and crowned with helmet-shaped glass bulbs cast light over bare trees and snow-dusted fields.

Edison's goal was to find an incandescent light that glowed at a steady rate, a clean, pure force. He added a filament to a vacuum, if you see what I mean. Am I making myself clear? It is important to me that you understand what I'm driving at.

If all this is still too oblique or elliptical you may wish to refer to the ending of Alfred Hitchcock's *Foreign Correspondent,* when the lights go out in the radio studio during the Blitz, and Joel McCrea calls into the mic: "Hello, America. Hang on to your lights. They're the only lights left in the world."

Or to the fires set by the Aborigines in the movie of *The Right Stuff.* At the high end of the dark, the light from the astronauts' capsule winks as it orbits the earth, while down here, the bonfires of the Aborigines glow white and spark.

Certain exceptional people are lights in winter. Louis Armstrong was one, especially when his eyes gleamed over the mouthpiece of his trumpet. Carole Lombard had a wit like sunshine. Fred Astaire was light on his feet.

Friends are lights in winter; the older the friend, the brighter the light. Teachers are, as well. One high school teacher of mine taught all there is to know of light and language. He died blind, out of the light. As did John Milton. "When I consider how my light is spent," Milton wrote, substituting light for life. "More light," said Goethe, as his was about to go out.

"This little light of mine. I'm gonna let it shine." I could sing that to you, if you like. Or I could recite "The Charge of the Light Brigade" (light reading). Bear with me. There's a bear with me. Yes, yes. I've told you that, too. Hang on. I'm coming to the point.

Not far from here a lighthouse tower rises over a channel where the bay opens to the Atlantic. It's not a tower really, more like a tall steel skeleton with a Cyclops eye circling at the top. It surveys the sea where, three hundred years ago, brave English sailors came to this area searching for a port. Without lights on the shore, they could not tell rocks and shallows from safe water. They had nothing to guide or protect them.

Which illustrates the fact that for winter lights to do their thing, there must be darkness and much cold around. Without that, they would be any old lights, and not the remarkable kind that rescues men in danger. Winter lights are heroes. But I hardly need to tell you, of all people, about that.

I bring you greetings from the long ago and our first snow together. Our eyes watered and our lips turned blue, but you refused to go inside. You said that the snow was meant for us alone, and so we stayed out until it got dark and darker still, and there was no light in the world but you.

ROGER ROSENBLATT's essays for *Time* and *The News-Hour* on PBS have won two George Polk Awards, the Peabody, and the Emmy. He is the author of six off-Broadway plays and seventeen books, including *New York Times* Notable Books *Kayak Morning* and *The Boy Detective*, as well as other national bestsellers *Unless It Moves the Human Heart*, *Making Toast*, *Rules for Aging*, and *Children of War*, which won the Robert F. Kennedy Book Prize and was a finalist for the National Book Critics Circle Award. He has held the Briggs-Copeland appointment in the teaching of writing at Harvard, and is currently Distinguished Professor of English and Writing at Stony Brook University. He lives in Quogue, New York.